Vedic Astrology:

The Light of Wisdom

Vedic Astrology:
The Light of Wisdom

Astrology for Beginners,

Learn the Language of Stars

Author

Ajay Srivastava

Jyotirvid, Jyotirvisharad

Copyright © Ajay Kumar Srivastava

Copyright No.: L-115439/2022

All rights reserved. No part of this publication may be reproduced, stored in a retrieval system, or transmitted in any form or by any means, electronic, mechanical, photocopying, recording, scanning, or otherwise, without the written permission of the author.

First Edition, 2023

Published by:

Ajay Kumar Srivastava

45, Awas Vikas Colony, Betiya Hata,

Gorakhpur – 273001 (U.P.), India

Mobile No.: +91-9867837184

Disclaimer: This publication contains the opinions and ideas of its author and is designed to provide useful information in regard to the subject matter covered. The author and the publisher specifically disclaim any responsibility for liability, loss, or risk, personal or otherwise, that is incurred as a consequence, directly or indirectly, of the use and application of any of the contents of this book.

Lord Ganesha

Prayer

ॐ नमो सिद्धि विनायकाय सर्व कार्य कर्त्रे सर्व विघ्न प्रशमनाय

सर्व राज्य वश्यकरणाय सर्वजन सर्वस्त्री पुरुष आकर्षणाय

श्रीं ॐ स्वाहा ।।

‖ Om Namo Siddhi Vinayakaya Sarva kaarya kartrey Sarva vighna prashamnay Sarvarjaya Vashyakarnaya Sarvajan Sarvastree Purush Aakarshanaya Shreeng Om Swaha ‖

(**Translation**: O Lord of Wisdom and Happiness, only you make every endeavor and everything possible. You are the remover of all obstacles and you have enchanted every being in the Universe, you are the Lord of all women and all men, Om Swaha.)

Dedication

I dedicate this book to my father (Late) Sri R.A.L Srivastava who taught me to be an independent, courageous and determined person, and my mother Maya Srivastava whose unconditional love and support always help me to overcome all the obstacles in my life. She has a selfless spirit and served others throughout her life. Her immense patience is peerless and she always inspires me to go ahead.

Preface

Astrology is the knowledge that shows the purpose of our existence as human beings on earth. This is a great science that has been given by our great sages and rishis for the benefit of humanity. Once upon a time in this country, the palace of astrology stood with full splendor and dignity. As time passed the castle began to fall, and the knowledge of astrology began to hide and went out of reach of the general public. Now the time is changing again and various astrologers are working hard, so that the great science could stand again in its full splendor. It is not a one-day job and every generation will have to contribute something so that astrology can stand with its full dignity again.

The ancient sages had written these formulas in codes so that people do not misuse them and do not misinterpret them. Great knowledge should always be in the right hands, those who have the capacity to decode these formulas can interpret this. Astrology is not just a predictive science; It is not a science to be used only for personal gain. One must be thirsty to find the truth of this existence before delving into the ocean of astrology.

Time is a great teacher, but it also throws dust on what is not prevalent or what we leave behind. Every now and then we need to hone our skills to stay sharp. Similarly, the knowledge which gets disappears now needs to be uncovered and sharpened. At present, there is a need for a new way of interpretation that is suitable for the changing world and new environment; there is a need for relevant examples which are suitable for the present generation so that people can understand the meaning behind the code written in our ancient texts.

Astrology has created a deep impact on my life. Once I was someone who didn't believe in astrology at all, and now I am writing a book on astrology. I remember the day January 27, 2017, at 5 pm; I started searching on the internet- "What is astrology?"

Later, I took admission in Bhartiya Vidya Bhavan, Mumbai, and started learning astrology. I am very grateful to the teachers of Bhavan who helped me a lot in clearing the various complicated concepts of astrology.

In this journey, I realized that there are many other people who want to learn astrology but they are unable to do so due to some constraints. I collected all my data and decided to write a book that will be beneficial for those who want to learn astrology from the very beginning.

I give special thanks to my younger brother Abhay Srivastava for their valuable suggestions, without which such work would not have been possible.

I bow to God for completing this book. The existence of this book is not possible without the grace of the Almighty.

Ajay Srivastava

13th February, 2022

Navi Mumbai

Acknowledgement

The existence of this book would not have been possible without the help of my wife Seema and my daughter Saanvi. They provided me enough help to write down my thoughts which I have collected so far in my life. My wife has been instrumental as an illustrator and proof-reader and has given me enough insights to write the matter in a simple and explanatory manner.

Ajay Srivastava

Contents

Chapter 1

Introduction

Vedic astrology is an ancient science of India. It deals with stars and planetary forces' effect on human beings. This knowledge has developed over thousands of years and various great sages and rishis have contributed in this field that how the universal forces affect the earth and what are the principles behind that.

The rotation of the earth and other planets around the Sun is not chaos, it is cosmos (the Greek word kosmos means "order") and everything whether it is a micro or macro is following a certain principle. These secrets are written in our texts called "Vedas" – which is "The Knowledge of the Supreme."

Every ancient civilization had some sort of system of beliefs that attributed the influence of planets and constellations to know the past, understand the present and predict the future. The human mind is always searching for the reason for their existence, from which source we have come to earth, and what is the reason behind this pain and sorrow in our life. Who will give the answer to all these questions, where is the light?

The name "Astrology" is having Greek roots and comes from the words "Astron" which means "Star" and "Logia" means "Study of". So, the word Astrology means "Study of Stars". Astrology in Sanskrit called "Jyotish" means "Jyoti" and "Isha" which means "Light" and "God". Hence, Jyotish means "The Light of God" or "The Science of Light".

Astrology is the study that everything that exists on earth has a meaningful purpose and we are not living in isolation in the universe. This human body is part of existence and the movement of celestial bodies affects us because the universe is full of energy and when the energy level changes due to the transit of planets, it not only affects our body but also the weather, geographical conditions, etc.

The study of astrology is vast and there are different branches of astrology. Most common we found it in newspapers and on television which is only for entertainment purposes. Serious astrology requires in-depth study of texts, scriptures, and some kind of intuition as predictions cannot be based only on mathematical calculations. Natal astrology is related to the horoscope calculated at the time of birth. Horary astrology determines the auspicious times for taking personal decisions. Mundane astrology studies the fate of countries, floods, earthquakes, weather, etc.

Astrology believes that everything on earth is controlled by celestial bodies otherwise predictions are completely impossible.

People are eager to know about the future events of their life but this is only a trivial worldly aspect. The true meaning of astrology is that one day the search will reach a level when we will know the reason for our existence and the whole play of the universe. Hence, astrology and spirituality are interconnected.

Our sages have discovered that planetary forces affect us and they contributed a lot to discover the truth behind it. The "Brihat Parashara Hora Shastra" written by Maharishi Parashar is the greatest treatise of astrology. The field was further contributed by Maharishi Brighu, Maharishi Jaimini, Mantreswara, Varahmihira, Vaidya Nath, Kalidas, Kalyan Verma, Ramanujacharya and many others made their great contributions in this field.

Vedic astrology believes in reincarnation and that the soul is immortal. Each soul bears the burden of its karma, and only we are responsible for all the happenings in our life. Here every action of us is being recorded and till we do not close our karmic account; we have to come time and again to settle the account.

The study of the birth chart prevents us from doing wrong deeds in this life. It gives us useful information about the timing of headwinds and tailwinds in our life so that we can take necessary measures and not get disheartened when the tide turns against us.

It does not mean that one should surrender to the hands of destiny rather it means that our destiny is in our hands - "You reap what you sow". It teaches us the value of patience in life, and once you realize it, the greatest secret is in your hands. Everything that happens in life is a gradual progress and the future is no different from the past, it comes from the past and no one can undo it.

A horoscope is the map of the sky at the time when a person has taken birth, the position of the planets in different signs holds the key to the assessment of events. Destiny is nothing but the results of our past karmas where fruits are delivered to us based on our past actions. Astrology says that for our every sorrow and happiness only we are responsible. So, we should not blame others for our misery and praise ourselves for our happiness because all these are our seeds that keep on turning into fruits from time to time. The study of "The Science of Light" helps us to disappear our ego, and accept that the Almighty is watching everything.

Lord Krishna says:

सर्वधर्मान्परित्यज्य मामेकं शरणं व्रज।

अहं त्वा सर्वपापेभ्यो मोक्षयिष्यामि मा शुच: ।।

(**Translation:** Abandon all varieties of religion and just surrender unto Me. I shall deliver you from all sinful reactions. Do not fear.)

Chapter 2

The Zodiac

The stars appear to move across the sky from the Earth and seem to be right next to each other in a constellation, but in reality, they are hundreds of light-years apart. The night sky looks a little different every night because the stars appear each night moving slightly west of where they were the night before. Our location on Earth also determines which stars and constellations we see, as the Northern Hemisphere is always pointing in a different direction than the Southern Hemisphere.

The Earth revolves around the Sun at a speed of about 30 km/sec and completes one revolution in 365.24 days, its period of rotation is 23.934 Earth hours. The rotation of the Earth has been gradually slowing down and a modern-day is longer by about 1.8 milliseconds than a century ago. As the Earth orbits the Sun, the Sun appears to pass in front of various constellations. The ecliptic is an imaginary line on the sky that marks the annual path of the Sun. The zodiac stretches about 9 degrees on either side of the ecliptic and is the region of the sky where we can find the Sun, Moon, and planets (except for Pluto). Astrology has divided the entire zodiac into 12 parts known as signs or rashis, because when the Earth revolved around the Sun, the Moon revolves around the Earth 12 times. The sidereal month of the Moon is 27.3 days and synodic month is 29.5 days and the Earth's orbit around the Sun is 365.25 days. So, the Moon orbits the earth 13.4 times relative to fixed stars (sidereal) and 12.4 times relative to the Earth (synodic).

Most of the constellations through which the ecliptic passes represent animals, the ancient Greeks called its zone "zôdiakos kyklos" which means "circle of animals" or "ta zôdia" means "the little animals". These twelve signs represent twelve bhavas, among them, ascendent is the most important, it represents our physical body and our journey started on this planet earth. The other two important bhavas are fifth and ninth, these three bhavas represent a rajasic, tamasic, and sattvic aspect of the soul.

2.1 Tropical and Sidereal Zodiac

The Tropical Zodiac

The zodiac system used in Western astrology is called the Tropical Zodiac which is based entirely on the Sun and the signs are set upon the ecliptic. The Tropical Zodiac is based on where the sun was stationed on each calendar day 2000+ years ago with knowledge pioneered by the ancient Babylonians, Egyptians, and Greeks. These cultures used the vernal or spring equinox (the time in spring when the sun crosses the equator, and when night and day are of equal length) as a reference to the beginning of the zodiac, 0° Aries. This system is not based on the stars but on the orientation of the Earth towards the Sun. In simple language, the zodiac became sealed in the sky, as the sky thousands of years ago, in the Tropical zodiac system.

The word "tropical" comes from the Greek "tropikos" meaning "turn". The Tropic of Cancer shows the location of the Sun on the summer solstice and the Tropic of Capricorn indicates the location of the Sun on the Winter Solstice.

The Sidereal Zodiac (Vedic System)

The sidereal sign tracks the movement of the Earth through the precession of the equinoxes. The word sidereal comes from the Latin word "sidus" which means "star or constellation". Outside the Solar System, the stars are stationary and appear as a 'steady' background for the moving planets.

The sidereal system considers the influence of stars outside the solar system. However, from the Earth's perspective, these fixed stars do actually move, the sky isn't fixed. The earth we know has a "wobble" is called the Precession of the Equinoxes. Over the course of thousands of years, the sky shifts, and the constellation the Sun once was in is no longer the same on a given day.

The Earth's axis is tilted 23.5 degrees from the plane of its orbit around the sun. But this tilt changes, the Earth's axis tilts one degree every 72 years and it takes 26,000 years in one cycle. Because this tilt changes, the season on earth also changes, more tilt means more severe seasons. The Earth's axis points towards the same direction in space as we orbit around the Sun, currently it points near Polaris and changes slowly with time. In the remote future (about 13,000 years) Vega will be the next North Star.

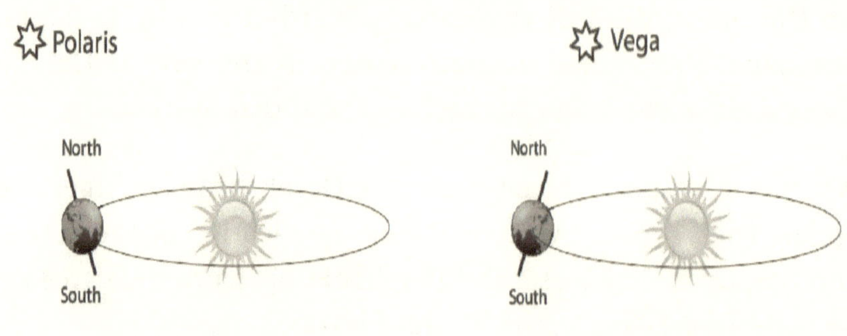

Polaris is the present north star.

Vega is the north star of the future.

2.2 Ayanamsha

The Tropical zodiac also called Sayana means "with Ayana". The Sidereal zodiac is also called Nirayana which means means "without Ayana". The difference between the tropical and sidereal zodiac is called the Ayanamsha.

Chapter 3

The Twelve Signs

The zodiac signs and the planets present in them indicate the physical features and characteristics of a person, health, finances, etc. A basic understanding of these signs is necessary before delving into the field of astrology. It is important to consider which planet is located in which sign and where is the lord of that sign situated? The element (Fire, Earth, Air, Water) of each sign, and due to the placement of planets, the weightage of which element is high is very important to consider. The native natural inclination is towards the characteristics of that element and his life forces will run accordingly. (Note - *Readers can find a detailed analysis of how the weightage of elements is calculated in my book, "Astrology & Predictions."*)

The placement and influence of the benefic and the malefic planets on these signs produce the results accordingly and affect the life of the native. In Hindu astrology, a person's zodiac is known by the presence of the Moon, but planets posited in other signs also affect his personality. Suppose a person's Moon is in Aries, then the person is considered to be of Aries, but if three planets are located in Libra, then the nature of Libra and the planets posited there also affect his personality and life.

Introduction of the Signs

3.1 Aries – The Ram

Key phrase - I Am

Aries is the 1st sign of the zodiac and extends from 0° to 30°. The constellations included in this zodiac are Ashwini, Bharani, and Kritika 1st pada. This sign is ruled by the red planet 'Mars – The God of War'. Therefore, Ariens are very courageous and dauntless. Sun gets exalted in this sign at 10° and Saturn gets debilitated at 20°.

The Symbol: The symbol of Aries is the Ram, which shows that they are impulsive, aggressive, and belligerent. They are ambitious and action-oriented people, full of vitality, always eager to explore new things, and not afraid to step into the unknown.

Jyotirlinga: The Jyotirlinga associated with Aries is Rameshwaram.

Classification: Aries is a positive, odd, and masculine sign. It is a fierce, rajasic, and movable sign. A rajasic sign represents a tendency to take action. The colour of the sign is red, an element is a fire, caste is Kshatriya and quality is dharma. It is a barren sign and is strong at night. It represents a forest or plateau and the direction is east. It is a Prishtodaya sign (rising with their hind part). It is a quadruped (four-legged) sign, indicating that they have a high ability to move forward and persevere when the going gets tough.

Characteristics: Ariens aspire to be the head of all affairs and do not like subordination. If this sign is strong and receives beneficial aspects, then they have good commanding power and can provide proper direction to others. When they recognize the opportunity, they can move forward against all odds with confidence. They are impulsive and lack the quality of patience. They have quick reactions and are not afraid to play with sharp objects. They are not afraid to try new things, take on new challenges, and want to take on another task before completing the first one.

Being the first sign of the zodiac, they have leadership qualities and are willing to take the initiative. They are entrepreneurial by nature and always aim high. The first sign represents initiation and newness; hence, they are the initiator of new things and the founder of the organization. It takes courage, vision, and high energy to start anything new and Ariens have that type of quality. The first sign also represents birth, innocence, and the beginning of the journey. They prefer to travel alone and do not wait for their companions, friends, and followers.

Being a positive sign of Mars, this energy acts as a protector and they are the best people to deal with a situation like an emergency. They have a strong ability to understand human psychology and are well versed in research and invention. They are very observant and have a scientific and logical mind which is full of new ideas. Two other fire signs, Leo and Sagittarius are their best companions.

This sign represents strong self-confidence, forceful character, thrust for their goal, and an uncompromising soul. Being a positive sign, they are ready to forgive others, they are outspoken have a clean heart, and do not like circumrotating matters. They never surrender and keep fighting till the end, their motto is – **"Success or death but no retreat"**. Mars, the lord of Aries, also rules over Scorpio, which is eighth from here and is also the house of transformation.

Therefore, Aries people's life is not stable and they get to see many changes. Being adventurous people, they keep moving from one place to another in search of new experiences.

Affliction: If the sign is afflicted, they are arrogant, quarrelsome, fierce, and boisterous. If more malefic influences the sign, then this energy will convert into obsession and they are ready to fight with anyone to fulfill their desire. They are explosive and may outburst on any matter. They behave like an autocrat and are not ready to listen to anyone's advice.

Body parts and diseases: Aries represents the head of the human body. They are prone to minor cuts and injuries, if more malefic is situated then serious accidents may be possible. They suffer from diseases like headache, eye problems, insomnia, brain-related problems, weak stomach, paralysis, etc.

3.2 Taurus – The Bull

Key phrase - I Have

Taurus is the 2nd sign of the zodiac and extends from 30° to 60°. The constellations included in this sign are Krittika 2nd, 3rd and 4th pada, Rohini and Mrigashirsha 1st and 2nd pada. The ruler of the sign is Venus and Moon is exalted here at 3 degrees.

The Symbol: The symbol of the sign is the bull. Like two bulls are good to pull a bullock cart, Taureans are very good to work in a team. Their synchronization is excellent with their team members, this makes them valuable employees for the organization.

Jyotirlinga: The Jyotirlinga associated with Taurus is Somnath (Gujarat).

Classification: It is an earthy and fixed sign. It is an even, auspicious and feminine sign. It is a negative sign, and its colour is white. It is a tamasic and vaishya caste sign and the quality of the sign is artha. It is a semi-fruitful sign and its direction is south. It represents a field or meadow. It is a prishtodaya sign (rises with back) and is strong at night. It is a quadruped (four-legged) sign.

Characteristics: Taureans have their principles and follow a practical path in their life. They are very devoted people and follow their traditions. They are straightforward, reliable, loyal, and creative people. They are faithful, trustworthy, persistent, and stable people. They have a strong sense of humour and are fond of pleasure. They have a strong sense of responsibility and work very diligently.

The sensitivity of Taureans is very high. They are emotional, sober, and romantic people. They don't run after relationships, but once it's done, they hold them for a long time, and they keep their promises. It is a highly fertile sign and a planet posited in Taurus feels highly comfortable and its productivity is high in this sign. Like, Ketu in Taurus, the native's inclination is toward religion and spiritual activities, and the native can easily remember religious doctrines. Venus in Taurus, the native can excel in Venusian pursuits easily.

Taureans have patience, are very honest, and work very hard. They are those people who have the strong capability to complete the unfulfilled task and never leave anything in between but they lack the initiation and aggression of Aries – which is the first sign of the zodiac.

Taureans are easily motivated by Venusian pursuits and want to enjoy the fruits of their labour. They are motivated by happiness and pleasure and like to enjoy parties, marriages, and other gatherings. They are very generous and like to invite friends for dinners. They are very cautious about their diet and correct nutrition is their first choice. They love cooking and gardening and plant beautiful creepers, flowers, plants, and trees.

Due to the Venus-ruled sign, they have an attractive face and an inclination towards Venusian qualities like singing, music, dance, etc. They are dress cautious people and always prefer to wear good-looking clothes. They communicate very well and like comfort and luxury in their life.

Being the second sign of the zodiac, it represents face and expressions, etc. It is also a house of family, wealth, and worldly possessions. Therefore, they are good in business, understand money-related matters very quickly and work hard to accumulate property.

Taurus is a quadruped sign; therefore, their movement is slow and sometimes they take a long time to complete the task but when fully charged their capacity is very high from others to move forward. They are perfectionists and due to the strong quality of patience, they are not ready to compromise easily and work hard for perfection. They are very liberal and broad-minded people and always ready to help others and even sometimes they forget their own money given to some other person.

Being an earthy sign, they prefer stability and don't like sudden changes in their life. They are very cautious people and prefer to put their feet back where there is any kind of insecurity. They are a valuable asset to the organization but when the organization is not ready to provide the stability and proper security for their future, they have no hesitation to leave such places. Taureans don't prefer to take a risk and prefer security in their life. Therefore, they prefer to do secure jobs and the temptation of big money does not attract them.

Like valuable assets, they are valuable people to their surroundings. They believe in hard labour, but sometimes they are very stubborn, lazy, and resistant to change. Due to stubbornness, they don't bother about other person's opinions and they don't change their opinion to please others. Their anger comes very slowly but once they are raged it is very difficult to control them. Sometimes their attitude is very dogmatic, which can lead to fierce anger and ready to destroy any obstruction.

Affliction: If the sign is afflicted then the person will become lazy and does not listen even after shouting. They are pleasure-seeking people and can take any wrong path to fulfill their desire, like overindulgence in sexual activities, drugs, etc. They are reserved, conservative, and egoistic people. They are covetous, may indulge to attain only physical pleasure, and will not give heed to any advice. Due to their stubborn nature, they are sometimes outright challenging to elders and superiors.

Body parts and diseases: The throat and neck are most susceptible to illness for Taureans. They may suffer from tonsils, diphtheria, pyorrhoea, etc.

3.3 Gemini – The Twins

Key Phrase – I Think

Gemini is the 3rd sign of the zodiac and extends from 30 to 90 degrees. The constellations included in this zodiac are Mrigashira 3rd and 4th pada, Ardra and Punarvasu 1st, 2nd, and 3rd pada. "Mercury – the messenger of the gods", rules this sign.

The Symbol: The symbol of the sign is Twins – a male and female joined together with the man holding a mace-like weapon and the woman playing a musical instrument (Veena).

Jyotirlinga: The Jyotirlinga associated with the sign is Nageshwara.

Classification: Gemini is an airy, satwic, dual, and positive sign. It is an odd, masculine, barren, and shudra caste sign. The colour of the sign is green and the quality of the sign is kama (desire). It lives in villages or bedrooms or a place for enjoyment and its direction is west. It is a bipeds (2 legged/ human) sign. It is a sheershodaya sign and is strong at night. The other two airy signs Libra and Aquarius are favourable with the sign and do quite well with Aries and Leo.

Characteristics: Geminis are skilled persons and they have a desire to create something new and explore new things. Mercury represents an intellectual personality with strong communication skills which can argue with logic and can offer his best advice. Being a dual sign, they are versatile. They are joyful but they are not easily satisfied and believe in change and in search of that they move from one place to another.

Geminis have sharp intelligence and their reaction is quick and witty. Being a dual sign, they can do more than one profession at a time. They are the person who can see both sides of the coin simultaneously. Therefore, they are best fitted with the job where negotiating skills are required. They are successful salespeople, brokers, and diplomats. They have a democratic attitude. The twin symbol indicates that they will show their best performance when they work together. Gemini is all about output, so they express their feelings externally while Virgo - the other sign ruled by Mercury, processes their emotions internally. Geminis are interested in writing reviews, love to chat, and while speaking they use their hands frequently.

Mercury represents a child who has an interest in asking questions. Mercury represents a merchant with strong business acumen, a merchant who is always looking to strike a fair deal, a merchant who does not reject an offer and loves to discuss first. Mercury represents strong intelligence, clear and logical thinking, penetrating vision, strong retention power, impulsive action, etc., Geminis have all such qualities.

They enjoy business conversation and are tactfully able to convert matters in their favour. They are liberal on the one hand and frugal on the other, both peculiar qualities present in their personality. They are inquisitive, like intelligent discussion and are good orators. They have excellent writing skills and talent in multiple languages. They are very curious people to seek all facts and figures before taking any action and keep asking questions till they get a clear idea to understand the matter. But sometimes, they behave like a highly timid and nervous person.

Gemini - The Twins, represents unification of masculine and feminine energy which gives birth to pure wisdom and provides immense possibilities for spirituality.

Affliction: They are a highly indecisive person and lack quality of concentration. They do not have patience and want to see the fruits of their work immediately. They are interested in shortcuts to achieve success and use their brain to dodge others. The shallow and wavering mind can convert into a cynic and eccentric person.

Body parts and diseases: This sign rules neck, arms, hands, and lungs. They easily suffer from cold and running noses. They suffer from pain in their hands, diseases in the neck and lungs. They suffer from T.B., Bronchitis, etc.

3.4 Cancer – The Crab
Key phrase – I Feel

Cancer is the 4th sign of the zodiac and extends from 90° to 120°. The constellations included in this zodiac are Punarvasu 4th pada, Pushya, and Aslesha. Moon is the lord of this zodiac and Jupiter is exalted here at 5° and Mars is debilitated at 28°.

The Symbol: The symbol of Cancer is a Crab. Crabs are found inland, pond, or well but not in deep water. Crab is eaten, they are very sensitive to noise and movement. People born under this sign are very sensitive; they are ready to sacrifice their life for any noble cause, for the betterment of their children and other family members. Crabs are decapods, meaning they have 10 legs and these legs are located in bilateral symmetry, with five on each side. It shows that Cancerians have very strong harmony and symmetry.

Jyotirlinga: The Jyotirlinga associated with Cancer is Omkareshwar.

Classification: Cancer is an auspicious and fruitful sign. It is a rajasic, negative and movable sign. It is an even, feminine and Brahmin caste sign. The colour of the sign is rosy or pink and the quality of the sign is moksha.

This sign represents pond or well and its direction is north. It is a keetapeds (reptiles) sign and is strong at night. It is a prishtodaya sign (rising with their hind part). The other two watery signs Scorpio and Pisces are favourable with this sign and do quite well with Taurus and Virgo.

Characteristics: Cancer is the first of the three water signs; its water is considered to be freshwater. Cancerians are very sensitive and emotional people. Just as a particle destroys the purity of water, they get easily hurt even by the loud voice of others. They are very kind and loving people but moody and peevish too. They are loyal and honest person. They are tenacious and feel strong bondage with their family and culture. They do not give up easily, once they have identified their goals. People born under this sign have a strong memory and a powerful intuition. They are deep observant and notice everything. They cover every minor detail and don't overlook anything. They are mysterious people who are not ready to open up easily, and keep everything to themselves.

They prefer a safe environment, a peaceful home, and a family life. They are looking for security first under any circumstances and want to remain in their shell if they sense any sign of danger. They are shy, non-aggressive person and do not believe in any kind of violence. They have a great desire to nurture and grow themselves and others.

Water can assume any shape depending upon the vessel, so they adapt to any situation. Being feminine and watery sign, they are very productive and produce great results if utilize their talent properly. Like water is not compressible, cancer-born people become rebellious when someone puts pressure on them, then they become very determined, stubborn, and outrageous.

Moon is the ruler of the sign represents the nurturing quality of the person. They are great teachers like a mother and able to provide proper guidance to others. They have a quick grasping ability and can produce new and innovative ideas. Like the waxing and waning Moon, Cancerians witness remarkable changes in their life. Being a movable and watery sign, they lead a wandering and restless life, experiencing many things and feeling life very deeply.

As the satellite of earth (Moon) movement is very fast, they are restless in nature and impatient. The exaltation of Jupiter signifies the protective nature of the sign while debilitation of Mars signifies the non-combative nature and inaction of this sign.

Affliction: If the sign is afflicted, they never forget their enemies and wait patiently for the right time to take revenge. They are very talkative and fickle-minded people. They are unable to take timely decisions and keep important files for a long time due to indecision, many times they miss opportunities due to inaction and indecisiveness.

Body parts and diseases: The body part associated with the sign is the heart and chest. Diseases they suffer from cough and cold, asthma, tuberculosis, infection of lungs, hysteria, etc.

3.5 Leo – The Lion

Key Phrase – I Create

Leo is the 5th sign of the zodiac and extends from 120 to 150 degrees. The constellations included in this zodiac are Magha, Purva phalguni and Uttara phalguni 1st pada. Leo is ruled by the Sun and it is also its Mooltrikona sign. No planets get exalted or debilitated here.

The Symbol: Leo's symbol is the Lion. It is a royal kingly sign. This represents the bold and courageous nature of Leonians. They tend to be daring and their speech is commanding. They have strong administrative abilities. They are noble and generous people and as a king, they are magnanimous and have a large heart.

Jyotirlinga: The Jyotirlinga associated with Leo is Vaidyanatha.

Classification: Among three fiery signs Aries, Leo, and Sagittarius, Leo is the middle. It is tamasic, positive and fixed sign. It is a hot, dry, barren, and fierce sign. It is an odd, masculine, and Kshatriya caste sign. The colour of the sign is pale-white and the quality is dharma. It is a quadruped sign (four-legged). This sign represents mountains or caves and the direction of the sign is east. It is a sheershodaya sign (rise with their head forward) and is strong in the day.

Characteristics: Leonians, being a sign of the Sun, have a great desire for creation and the will to live. There is no life on earth without Sun, when Sun rises darkness disappears. Worship of the Sun removes ignorance and evil thoughts. Leonians take very much interest in creative activities and join those organizations which are helpful to mankind.

A positive, and fire sign represents thrust for knowledge and they are always ready to learn. They are frank and broad-minded person. On the other hand, they are blunt and outspoken, therefore, they have fewer friends.

Fire and fixed signs represent a high level of energy. They are like a young adult who has confidence in their ability and are ready for action. They are a warm, passionate and charismatic person. They are extroverts with full of fun. They have dignity, hate getting their hands dirty, and prefer to get others to do such kind of work. They are a very honest person and it is difficult to question their integrity. They are an intelligent and hard-working person and learn in art and culture. They want to live a free life and hate any kind of boundation.

Leonians are self-centred and ambitious people. They are choosy in relationships. Like a father protecting his family, they feel a responsibility to protect their surroundings. They help people voluntarily and do charity. They never hesitate to help their friends and are ready to give up their comfort when needed. Prestige and honour are of great importance for them and they are willing to maintain it at any cost even when they are in a state of scarcity. They are very cautious about their dress, curtains, and furniture and keep their home tidy. They are extravagant and want to live lavishly; therefore, they face tough times in life due to poor savings.

Planets in this sign represent the leadership quality of the person and a sense of showmanship. They have a desire to be seen and display their talent to the world. Planets in Leo represent a person who wants to be independent and attract attention, admiration, and respect from others. Sun in Leo represents that the person has leadership quality, fewer friends, and live a lonely life. Mountain or caves represents the isolation and silence of the sign. They do not talk much and hate worthless discussions. They listen to every opinion, don't ignore rumors, and make decisions wisely.

Sun always moves in forward motion and never retrogrades. They are known for their determination, bravery, loyalty, stability, and consistency.

Lions have terrific night vision and are most active at night; therefore, Leonians find themselves comfortable at night work without any sign of lethargy. Early morning wake-up is not a problem for Leonians. Lions are ready to fight to protect their food, so Leonians are ready to fight when needed. They lead a disciplined life and spend most of their lives in one place.

Affliction: If the sign is afflicted, they become highly arrogant and aggressive person. They are short-tempered and feel hurt by any trivial matter. They are conservative and stubborn; dormant and stupid; harsh and tough; tyrant and ruthless. They have an urge for recognition and an excessive desire to be special.

Because of their pride, they are susceptible to flattery and by exaggerating their ego sycophants use this weakness.

Body parts and diseases: Among body parts, Leo indicates heart, stomach, and back. Diseases related to heart diseases, pain in the back and ribs, headache, fever, smallpox, measles, jaundice, inflammations, etc.

3.6 Virgo – The Virgin

Key Phrase – I Analyze

Virgo is the 6th sign of the zodiac and extends from 150° to 180°. The constellations included in this sign are Uttara phalguni 2nd, 3rd, and 4th pada, Hasta and Chitra 1st, and 2nd pada. Gemini and Virgo are the own signs of Mercury, but Virgo is its Mooltrikona sign and it gets exalted here at 15°.

The Symbol: Virgo sign symbol is a virgin girl standing in a boat carrying grains and fire in her hands. This virgin sign represents feminine aspects of 'Nature'. Virginity represents cleanliness and purity. If Mercury is strong in a chart, it can produce new and innovative ideas. Fire is the symbol of knowledge, this symbol shows that they are not easily satisfied with superficial observation and they have great capacity for in-depth analysis.

Jyotirlinga: The Jyotirlinga associated with this sign is Mallikarjuna.

Classification: Among three earthy signs; Taurus, Virgo, and Capricorn, Virgo is the second. It is an auspicious, even, and female sign. It is a sattwic, negative and dual sign. The quality of the sign is artha (wealth) and caste is vaishya (merchant). It is a barren sign and strong during the day. The colour of the sign is variegated or piebald. This sign represents land with water and cultivated vegetation. The direction of the sign is south. It is a bipeds (2 legged/ human) sign. It is a sheershodaya sign (rises with their head forward).

Characteristics: The rulership of Mercury on this sign represents an analytical mind, intelligence, and strong business acumen. This sign is capable of producing great business leaders but they also have to go through tough phases of life. They have strong potential for creation. They like to cooperate with others and are very good at teamwork. They use their intellect to win debates, good critics and are strong in negotiations. They have clear concepts and can present disorganized data in an organized manner. They want to finish one task first before starting the other.

Mercury is a fast-moving planet, which indicates inconsistency. They like to travel and move from their birthplace. They are quick in action and often change their residence and jobs. They are shy and sensible people. They are discerning, patient, careful, and meticulous people.

They are practical and detail-conscious people. They are soft-spoken people and always keep lovely smiles on their faces. They are a smart, active person and look younger than their age. They are conscious about their physique and keep control of their tummy.

Earthy signs represent reliability and stubbornness. They are hardworking and conscientious people. They keep a strong grip on their holding and take care of their belongings. Their secret savings no one knows and they are good at saving money. They never reveal their secrets to anyone. They like gardening and agriculture.

Being a dual sign, they look for alternate possibilities and focus on alternate sources of income. They keep back up of their important items. They adjust themselves as per the situation when necessary. They are perfectionists, every task after completion they check it again which reduces the chances of mistakes and increases their perfection.

As Leos prefer to show their talent to the world, Virgoans prefer to develop their talent, one after another. This is the sign where the best logical and spiritual exploration of the universe begins and they have an insatiable desire to quest for the truth.

Affliction: If the sign is afflicted, they are an argumentative and illicit pleasure-seeking person. They use their brain to take undue advantage and become scammers and hackers. They are cunning, clever thieves, shrewd statisticians, etc.

Body parts and diseases: Among body parts, Virgo indicates the area of the abdomen. They are more susceptible to bowel trouble and indigestion than other diseases. They easily fall victim to diseases like loose motion, diarrhoea, dysentery, other stomach ailments, etc.

3.7 Libra – The Man with a Scale

Key Phrase – I Balance

Libra is the 7th sign of the zodiac and extends from 180° to 210°. The constellations included in this zodiac are Chitra 3rd and 4th pada, Swati and Vishakha 1st, 2nd, and 3rd pada. Venus is the lord of this sign and it is also its Mooltrikona Sign. Saturn gets exalted here at 20° and Sun is debilitated at 10°.

The Symbol: This sign is represented by a man walking in a market carrying a scale of balances.

Jyotirlinga: The Jyotirlinga associated with this sign is Mahakaleshwar.

Classification: Libra is an airy, rajasic, and masculine sign. It is a positive and movable sign. It is an odd and fierce sign. This sign represents busy town or marketplace. It is a semi-fruitful sign and the direction of the sign is west. The colour of the sign is black, the quality of the sign is kama (desire) and the caste is shudra. It is a sheershodaya sign (rise with their head forward) and is strong during the day. It is a biped (2 legged/ human) sign.

Characteristics: Librans are those people who always make balance in their relationships. They are looking for harmony, impartiality, and justice with everyone. They always look neat and clean and dislike dirty work of any kind. They are a charming, sensible, modest, gentle, and spendthrift person.

Market place represents these people have the strong business capability. They are diplomatic and interested in their gains but do not like arguments of any kind. They speak the truth and are not interested in making profits by deceiving others. They do not show their anger but create their impact. They are not easily satisfied and being a movable sign, they search here and there for excellence. They like to compromise but don't want to indulge in a fight in any controversial matters. They want to buy peace at any cost and are ready to pay more for that. In any type of quarrel, they prefer not to indulge, keep their mouth close and start avoiding the situation.

Librans are tall and graceful people with a smile on their faces. They are a very social person and very active on social media platforms. They like to comment on social media posts. Being an airy sign of Venus, they are very popular among their friends and pay attention to everyone. They are rarely loners, they have a strong urge for a partner, and therefore, it is very difficult to find any Librans unmarried.

They can't live alone because the market is the expansion of "two". They prefer taking pictures with their partner and posting them on social media rather than taking them alone. The market also requires someone with strong legs, as you often have to move from one place to another. Therefore, Librans have strong legs and can't sit still for long. To fulfill their desires, they have to travel from place to place, and they have to meet a variety of people for business, and all these qualities are reflected in this sign.

The symbol of the scale of balance represents mental equilibrium and they can see the merits and demerits of an issue. Before concluding, they judge all pros and cons of the situation. Therefore, they are the best balancer and good counsellor. A career that involves deciding on taking a review of the situation brings them success. They can handle tough situations and do not lose their mental balance. But sometimes such quality creates a problem, among too many pros and cons they take much time to take any decision.

Venus ruling of this sign represents a realm of materiality. A positive sign of Venus represents creative qualities like poetic abilities, art, music, dance and drama, philanthropic activities, etc. Venus indicates they are dress-conscious people, like perfumes, properly keeping their documents and files, and live-in beautiful surroundings. They work as musicians, designers, artists, and fashionistas. They are a very hard-working person and want to enjoy all comforts and luxuries of life. They like romantic music and enjoy much in the company of the opposite sex.

Planets in Libra represent that the person is polite in his behaviour, etiquettes and manners are their priorities. They have strong dancing capability and can balance their body swiftly. This sign represents the dancing posture of Lord Shiva – "Nataraja". They are always engaged in good deeds, listen to other person's problems very carefully and sometimes they take pain themselves to help others.

The airy sign represents brilliance and intellect. They are a smart and clever person but not cunning. They are trained and skilled in many arts. They have clear thoughts and can present them in front of others. They like to create an atmosphere of peace and act with consideration. Their decisions are unbiased and they do not favour nepotism.

The opposite side of Libra is Aries which represents that on the top of the mountain person is alone; while Libra - the marketplace, represents the popularity of the person and likes to mingle with others. For Aries **'Spirit'** is of great importance but for Libra **'Matter'** is prime. The zodiac sign "Scales" represents the balance between the material and spiritual worlds. A perfectly balanced zodiac sign provides a person with luxuries but does not allow them to enjoy them. Therefore, people born under this sign should avoid any kind of overindulgence as Saturn, the lord of karma, is exalted here, which balances everything.

Affliction: The afflicted sign represents disharmony, unbalanced, perturbed, anxious, tense, and upset nature. It is very difficult for Librans to stay alone. A period of loneliness or isolation is like hell for them. They need motivation in their difficult phase of life. Due to too much consideration, they lack the quality of decisiveness and they need to develop to take prompt decisions. They lack the quality of patience and need to learn to wait.

Body parts and diseases: Libra indicates below the navel and hips. They are prone to stomach-related problems, suffer from muscle disorders, joint pains, diabetes, leprosy, defect in the kidney, problems in the uterus for ladies, pain in the spines, etc.

3.8 Scorpio – The Scorpion

Key Phrase – I Desire

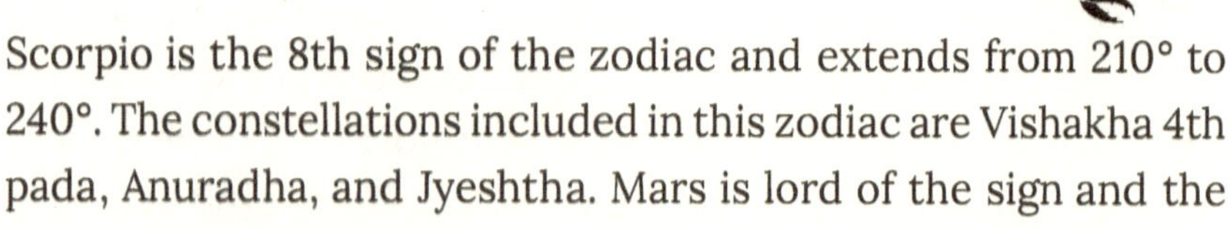

Scorpio is the 8th sign of the zodiac and extends from 210° to 240°. The constellations included in this zodiac are Vishakha 4th pada, Anuradha, and Jyeshtha. Mars is lord of the sign and the Moon gets debilitated here at 3°. Ketu is the co-ruler of the sign.

The Symbol: The symbol of Scorpio is the scorpion. Scorpions hide under logs, rocks, and wet places where moisture and temperature are suitable. Scorpions are tough, fierce, and ruthless hunters. Their patience for their prey is tremendous. They have a strong capacity to sit for hours at one place waiting for victims to come to close. They are most active during the night and wait at their burrow to ambush their prey. Scorpions like wet and watery places and can climb any top if the desired object is there. The tail of scorpions which is filled with poison represents an interest in chemistry, drugs, poison, death, and the occult.

Jyotirlinga: The Jyotirlinga associated with Scorpio is Grishneshwar.

Classification: Scorpio is an auspicious, negative, and fixed sign. It is a watery and tamasic sign. It is a fruitful sign and strong during the day. It is a brahmin, feminine, and even sign. The colour of the sign is golden and the quality is moksha. This sign represents a hole or cavity, a hiding place. It is a keetapeds (reptiles) sign and the direction is north. This sign makes the best compatibility with Cancer and Pisces.

Characteristics: Scorpios have inherent probing quality and strong imagination and intuition. Their research capability and investigation power are strong and they like to penetrate secrets but prefer to remain behind the scenes. They have a great understanding of the human mind and a strong capacity to unfold the mystery. To solve the mystery, they collect the information from every nook and corner and absorb every bit of information. They do not trust easily to anyone and like to investigate one thing from various aspects. They become good investigators or detectives. They can easily find those hidden things which are difficult and not very obvious to others.

The nature of water is fluid and where it flows it adapts to the nature and shape where it falls. But when it is fixed it becomes murky. When water is stagnant at a place it starts going deep.

Therefore, this sign represents deep emotions, underneath the surface and hidden things. Being a fixed watery sign, these natives have strong control of their emotions. This is a sign of transformation; they have great potential to transform themselves and others. A brahmin caste sign represents they work as a healer. Medicine and surgery are also represented by this sign.

They have a strong capability to survive in difficult circumstances. They are persistent and determined to achieve the desired object. They work for long hours and are ready to sacrifice anything for their purpose. Their memory is excellent; they remember everything and never forget even after years. They easily remember all the facts and can bring them to the table when necessary. Their strike is sudden and in arguments, they can surprise the opponents with facts and figures.

Scorpio is the negative sign of Mars. Hence, the malefic nature of Mars; arrogance, autocratic temperament, conflict, chaos, and destruction are also visible here. They are very stubborn and do not care about criticism. Due to their stubbornness, they don't like a question on their opinion. They can speak for hours and others are there only to listen to them. They believe that they are always right and being a fixed sign, they don't see any reason to change their view. Due to their strong fighting spirit, they never accept defeat and are not ready to compromise under any circumstances. They cannot easily give up and fight for anything which obstructs their desired goal.

Scorpio is the darkest of all the constellations and is related to hidden aspects of life. Therefore, dark, secret and hidden things naturally attract them and they don't want to reveal much about themselves. Scorpio people are so deep that it is very difficult for others to understand them. You can never anticipate the next move of a Scorpio person even after living with them for years. All their actions are in deep silence and they have a great capacity to imbibe all the secrets.

They are extremists, once they have set their goal, they rush to achieve it without wasting a second. They work hard, have intense dedication, and often become workaholics. They are power, position, and money-hungry people. When they are in a power position, they can fire people immediately even the most trusted person without giving any notice.

Scorpio water is muddy water; therefore, for their greed and benefit, they manipulate things. They can manipulate others emotionally as well for their benefit. They say something but deep down they do not follow the same. They keep the important papers underneath the table and wait for even years and take decisions only when the situation turns in their favour and do not bother about others' sufferings.

On the higher aspect, it is the sign of occult, mysticism, secret knowledge, kundalini, and spirituality. The continuous fighting spirit represents till the attainment of "The Ultimate Truth" they will not surrender. This sign's transformation reflects a shift from lower genital pleasures to higher spiritual mysteries. It is the only sign of the zodiac that has strong potential for both good and evil. With such high energy, the native has the capacity to reach either zenith or nadir depending on their karmas.

Affliction: If the sign is afflicted, extreme passion and obsession are also visible. They are rude and cruel in nature and sex-obsessed. They are unreliable and have a connection with illicit people. This sign represents the cunning, revengeful, and relentless nature of a person. They view everyone with suspicion and never accept food offered. They flatter their superiors, eager to form relationships with powerful people, but look down on their juniors and the weak. Because they are hungry for power and money they never hesitate to adopt any unfair means to obtain it.

After getting hurt even by a small thing, they do not forgive and take revenge when the time comes and do not bother about repercussions. They change their decisions at the last minute, disregarding the consequences or the pain of others. They have a controlling attitude towards others and do not like rebellion.

They are highly jealous and possessive and due to this reason their relationship turns bad. They like to live alone but their craving for a partner is always there who can understand them better. Their nature is stingy and due to the virile Martian energy, they feel pleasure while beating others.

They react very sharply when met with any obstruction from outside. Their hidden and ugly nature is not easily manifested if their feeling is not wounded. This cunning, vindictive nature is fuelled by a strong tendency to hurt not only their opponents but also those they love most.

Body parts and diseases: The sign rules the secrets and genitals parts of the human body, bladder, prostate gland, womb, ovaries, etc. They suffer diseases like fistulas, all secret and virtual diseases, ruptures, obstructions of the intestinal canal, problem-related to the liver, etc.

3.9 Sagittarius – The Archer (Half Man, Half Horse)

Key Phrase – I see

Sagittarius is the 9th sign of the zodiac and extends from 240° to 270°. The constellations included in this zodiac are Mula, Purva Ashadha, and Uttara Ashadha 1st pada. Jupiter – the planet of expansion and good fortune rules this sign, it is also its Mooltrikona Sign. No planets get exalted or debilitated here.

The Symbol: The sign is represented by a Centaur – half man and half horse - holding a bow and shooting an arrow.

Jyotirlinga: The jyotirlinga associated with the sign is Kashi Vishwanath.

Classification: It is a fiery, sattwic, and masculine sign. It is a semi-fruitful, and dual sign. It is a positive, odd, and fierce sign. This sign represents villages, cities, treasuries, or military posts and the direction of the sign is east. The colour of the sign is yellow, the quality is dharma and the caste is kshatriya. It is a prishtodaya sign (rising with their hind part) and is strong at night. This sign is bipeds (first half) and quadruped (second half).

Characteristics: This fiery sign indicates enthusiasm, ambition, and aspiration. They are fearless and confident people; they are not the ones to run away from a bad situation and are ready to face any situation without any fear. They are wanderers and have a strong desire to increase their knowledge and outlook towards the world. They are born to explore, and the quest for truth knows no bounds for Sagittarians. They do courageous acts that others hesitate to do. They work on innovative ideas that no one had thought of before and they like to visit new places that others are afraid to go. The more they explore they find that the more exciting world waits for further exploration.

They are philosophical and like to study religious literature and maintain a mini library at home. Like Arjun of Mahabharat, they show their best talent in difficult circumstances. They are not impulsive like Arians and take proper decisions after careful deliberation. They are not in a hurry and delay their plans when they find that planning is not satisfactory. Jupiter is considered an advisor; therefore, they like to advise others. They harmonize best with Arians and Leonians.

Being a Positive and Satwik sign they like only truth. A fierce and fiery sign represents energy, zeal, vigour, passion, and vitality. They fight for justice and being a Kshatriya sign they are ready to pull their sword if they found any injustice is done not only for him but for others also. They are the man of their word and stick with their principles even if the final result would not favourable for them. They speak harsh truth in front of others without any hesitation. Therefore, it is good to discuss any matter in private with Sagittarians.

This dual sign represents a transformation of the person from the beast (half-horse) to the human being (half-man). They become nobler in their life and take interest in spiritual activities. But any transformation is not easy, they have to face various turmoil and challenges in their life. Being a sign of human and animal, their approach is humanitarian. They prefer to visit forests rather than a garden, meaning the allure of traveling into the unknown draws them in. They prefer playing outdoor games rather than indoor games.

Due to the fiery sign of Jupiter, they do not like the orders of others. If people politely say so and request them to do so, then they do. They perform better when they have a free hand and no one hinders their decision-making. They are an intuitive person and have good retention power. They are true friends and offer all kinds of help when their friends need it. The 9th house is the house of religion, higher education, and long travel. Planets in the sign represent a person who will take interest in religious activities, higher education, and do long travel.

Affliction: If the sign is afflicted, they lack tact, are not a trustworthy person, and keep false promises. They are fanatics, narrow-minded people, and start the following someone blindly.

Body parts and diseases: Among body parts Sagittarius rules hips, thighs and buttocks. They are prone to injuries to the hips and thighs. They suffer from rheumatic pain, diabetes, etc.

3.10 Capricorn – The Goat

Key phrase – I Utilize

Capricorn is the 10th sign of the zodiac and extends from 270° to 300°. In Hindu astrology, the Sanskrit term Makara is equivalent to the Zodiac sign Capricorn - refers to a crocodile. The constellations included in this zodiac are Uttara Ashadha 2nd, 3rd, and 4th pada; Sharavana and Dhanishta 1st and 2nd pada. Saturn is the lord of this zodiac.

Mars gets exalted in this sign at 28° and Jupiter gets debilitated at 5°. In India, on every calendar day of 14th or 15th January, we celebrate Makar Sankranti, when Sun enters in this sign. This is the only festival in the country that celebrated on a specific day according to the solar calendar, instead of other festivals which is celebrated as per the lunar calendar.

The Symbol: Capricorn is represented by the sea-goat, a mythological creature with the body of a goat and the tail of a fish.

Jyotirlinga: The Jyotirlinga associated with Capricorn is Bhimashankar.

Classification: It is an auspicious and earthy sign. It is a negative, rajasic, and movable sign. It is an even, feminine, and semi-fruitful sign. The quality of this sign is artha, and the caste is vaishya. It is a prishtodaya sign (rises with back) and is strong at night. Its direction is south. Its colour is brownish or variegated. It represents forests with plenty of water. The first half of this sign is a quadruped and the second half is footless. The four legs on earth show that during the first half it moves very slowly but a long tail in the second half shows it moves in the water with dignity and pace.

Characteristics: They are very sincere and honest people. Being an earthy sign and ruled by the Saturn, security is the top priority for them and they avoid taking any kind of risk. They focus only on realistic matters. They don't like to live in dreams and hate to discuss impractical ideas, even if it sounds good to others. In a meeting, they try to remain silent if they are unable to avoid such types of discussions. They are curious and good at planning, practical but stubborn and conservative. They scrutinize the documents very carefully and to investigate any matter, they want to go deep.

Capricorn is the strongest earth sign among the other earthly signs -Taurus and Virgo, which indicates that there are high limits and restrictions. The key phrase of this sign is 'I Utilize' indicates that this sign has a very strong capacity to make full use of available resources. Energy is useful only when it is utilized properly. In this sign, the planet of energy Mars is exalted, which shows that it has a strong power to control and fully utilize energy. Jupiter representing expansion (Aakash-Sky), feels hapless in this sign due to excessive restrictions and is debilitated here.

The planets in this sign indicate that they are very economical and do not like to waste anything. They use all available resources very carefully. They don't like to speculate and invest only in a solid profession after deep scrutiny. They don't shy away from rolling up their sleeves and getting their hands dirty to complete the task and create something incredible. It shows that the person has a strong determination to achieve his goal in life. They have a strong ability to work for long hours without any distractions.

The symbol of the goat represents the sacrificial nature of this sign. The goat has a strong ability to reach the top of the hill amidst various difficulties. Therefore, this symbol represents the ability for an ambitious climb to the top and quiet endurance. They do not trust others and make their way. They are very hardworking and have a strong sense of fulfillment of their duty. They want to enjoy all the luxuries of life and they have a strong ability to work hard to achieve them.

Being a feminine sign and ruled by Saturn, they tend to preserve anything before it goes bad. They are reserved in nature and want to be aloof from others and do not make friends easily. Saturn also represents hindrances, obstacles, and slow movement. The planets in Capricorn indicate that a person has to face all these things in his life but success will come only if he does not leave it.

Affliction: If the sign is afflicted it is very difficult for them to change their conservative thoughts. They are dishonest, miser, greedy, and lethargic. Too much malefic in this sign indicates that the person will not hesitate to commit any crime.

Body parts and diseases: Among the body parts, Capricorn is related to the knees - which signifies the 'support and movement' of this sign. Injury near the knee cap, dislocation, rheumatism, hysteria, diseases related to cold, etc.

3.11 Aquarius – The Waterman

Key phrase - I Know

Aquarius is the 11th sign of the zodiac and extends from 300° to 330°. The constellations included in this zodiac are Dhanishta 3rd and 4th pada, Shatabhisha and Purva Bhadrapada 1st, 2nd, and 3rd pada. Saturn is the lord of this zodiac and Rahu is the co-ruler. Aquarius is the Mooltrikona sign of Saturn. In Western astrology, Aquarius is ruled by Uranus.

The constellation of Aquarius is located near other water-related constellations, often called the water or sea segments of the sky – such as Cetus - the whale, Pisces - the fish, Delphinus - the dolphin, and Eridanus - the river. In a geometric symbolic presentation, Aquarius is represented by two wavy zig-zag lines which show a strong relation of water or electricity with this sign.

The Symbol: Aquarius symbol is a man pouring a water pot. Aquarius is coming from the Latin word "Aquarii" which means "water carrier" and in Sanskrit, it is called Kumbha which means pitcher. The symbol of pouring water represents the humanitarian nature of this sign.

Jyotirlinga: The Jyotirlinga associated with the sign is Kedarnath.

Classification: Aquarius is an airy, tamasic, and fixed sign. It is an odd and masculine sign. It is a positive, semi-fruitful, and fierce sign. Its colour is dark brown. It is a shudra caste sign and represents kama (desire). It is a biped sign (2 legged/human). It represents villages and its direction is west. It is a sheershodaya sign (rises with their head forward) and strong in a day.

Characteristics: Aquarians are very social and always try to bring harmony among people but due to the effect of Saturn, they are silent workers. They have their individuality and specialty but due to fixed signs, they do not allow others to enter their circle. Being an airy sign, Aquarians have a great capacity to understand and connect every type of concept and person. Due to fixed sign, they are looking for long-lasting relationships, but they are stubborn and like to stick to their principles.

They have strong patience but they achieve success only after persistent effort. Therefore, they are suitable for research work and for those works where multiple efforts are required. They have a scientific mind and like to research on this line.

Due to the airy sign, they are extremely intelligent and their approach is very practical. They are very idealistic and kindness is in their heart, therefore, they always prefer to support the downtrodden in the society and prefer to work that has humanitarian benefits. They are very sincere and honest and their likes and dislikes are very strong. Being an airy sign, they have a good harmony with the other two airy signs Gemini and Libra. The quality of the sign is desire (kama); therefore, they have a strong desire for material gain but they are not greedy. They work very hard for what they want but are not willing to take a single pie that is not for their share.

Freedom and independence are the Aquarians' keywords because it is an airy sign and are ruled by Saturn. They prefer friendship and teamwork, but they also need time to be alone for some time to rejuvenate themselves. Because it is a fixed sign, they have strong opinions and don't go back down from an argument. They have a strong ability to see both sides of a coin which makes them excellent problem-solvers. Planets in this sign, show that the person prefers their individuality and doesn't like to interfere with any person.

Due to the element of air and relation with water they are very deep thinkers and have strong retention power. With their penetrating eyes, they can read the hidden motives of others and they hate flattery and hypocrisy. They are very adaptable to the situation and capable of conquering boundaries.

Co-rulership of Uranus represents; occult, radical changes, revolution, innovation, technology, and surprising events. It is a fixed sign ruled by Saturn, so they are very lazy people and do not move from their place even after shouting a lot. On the positive side, they have a strong ability to sit in a place for long periods of time, have strong powers of concentration and can become true seekers of truth who sit in deep meditation at one place.

Affliction: Sometimes it seems that everything is in their head on the other hand sometimes they are very moody, eccentric, rebellious, and unconventional. The afflicted air element in this sign results in disharmony or break up in a long relationship.

Body parts and diseases: Aquarius is associated with the shins, ankles, and circulatory system. An air-related problem in the body; gout, cramp, rheumatism, pain in the leg, lameness, and diseases produced from foul blood, etc.

3.12 Pisces – The Fishes

Key phrase – I Believe

Pisces is the 12th sign of the zodiac and extends from 330° to 360°. The constellations included in this zodiac are Purva Bhadrapada 4th pada, Uttara Bhadrapada, and Revati. In this sign, Venus is exalted at 27° degree and Mercury is debilitated at 15°.

The Symbol: Its symbol is fish (two fish move in opposite directions, one towards the north and the other towards the south).

Jyotirlinga: The Jyotirlinga associated with the sign is Trimbakeshwar.

Classification: Pisces is a watery, sattwic, and dual sign. It is an auspicious and negative sign. It is an even, feminine, and fruitful sign. The colour of the sign is white, the cast is Brahmin and the quality is moksha (nirvana). It is a keetapeds (reptiles) sign and its direction is north. This sign represents places with water and is strong during twilight.

Characteristics: Pisces is ruled by Jupiter which represents philosophy, knowledge, and wisdom. Under the influence of Jupiter, Pisces people are honest people and try to avoid any kind of conflict. They are not combative and do not like to participate in cut-throat competitions. They act as a mediator among many tussles. Due to a feminine sign, they are a very modest person and always behave in a very polite manner. Due to their truthiness, they easily believe in their friends but later regret, because they forget that there are not only true human beings but also evil ones present in this world and it is not always good to trust everyone.

They never leave any work in the middle and try to complete it before taking on any new task. They have a sharp memory and being a watery sign, they adapt to any kind of situation. They are kind and are very loyal people. They are also very moody persons and if Moon is afflicted in a person's birth chart, they are always indecisive and unable to make timely decisions.

They tend to forgive their enemies but when they are angry, they easily withdraw their shield of help from others. The exaltation of Venus here indicates that they are very good at advisory services. The feminine qualities of receptivity, sense of security, and parenting are visible here. They are very sensitive people and can capture the hidden thoughts and feelings of others.

The key phrase – 'I believe' shows they tend to have beliefs on their feelings and intuitions. Among three watery signs Cancer, Scorpio and Pisces; Pisces water is ocean water which represents depth in their personality. They are cold and wet, and in the winter season, they feel very cold compared to other people.

In western astrology, Pisces is co-ruled by the planet Neptune (God of the Ocean) which represents idealists, imagination, illusion, escapism, and mysticism.

On the higher side, it represents visionaries, glamorous and charismatic personalities. For Pisceans dreams, myths and fantasies feel more real than ordinary life. Like a fish in an ocean, they are a very creative and movable person but feel like a fish out of water when their creativity is not used.

This 12th sign is the last sign of the zodiac, the journey that started from Aries is going to end here now, this is the sign of salvation. Therefore, they have a strong desire for spirituality and want to study astrology and other occult sciences. A strong sign produces great artists and creative personalities and some time in life they delve into the ocean of spiritualism.

Affliction: On a day of thick fog over the sea, it is difficult to look ahead and differentiate between the sea and the sky. That shows illusionary, day-dreamers, and away from reality if this sign is afflicted. To escape from their boring mundane life, they may indulge in alcohol and drugs or may indulge in other wrong ways and try to forget their misery. They are slow to react and tend to have a lethargic type of personality.

Body parts and diseases: Pisces is related to the feet and toes which represents the supportive nature and movement of the person and they are able to bear heavy responsibility without any complaint. If this sign is afflicted in the birth chart of the native, then the person may have problems related to feet at some point of time in life.

3.13 Summary of Important Characteristics of the Signs

I) Elements of Signs

a) Fire Sign (Agni)

- The fire signs are: Aries, Leo and Sagittarius (1,5,9)

- Extrovert, Deeply Compassionate, Restless, Energetic, Action-oriented, Optimistic, Assertive, Inspirational, Independent, Freedom-loving and Leadership quality

b) Earth Sign (Pruthvi)

- The Earth signs are: Taurus, Virgo and Capricorn (2,6,10)

- Practical, Trustworthy, Reserved, Strong sense of duty, Conservative, Stubborn, Persistent and Hardworking

c) Air Sign (Vayu)

- The Air signs are: Gemini, Libra and Aquarius (3,7,11)

- Intelligent, Idealistic, Communicators, Sociable, Independent, Restless, Critical thinkers, Curious, Inquisitive and Mentally active

d) Water Sign (Jal)

- The Water signs are: Cancer, Scorpio and Pisces (4,8,12)

- Deep observant, Perceptive, Adaptable, Emotional, Sensitive, Indecisive, Intuitive and Mysterious

e) Space (Aakash)

- There are no space signs

- Jupiter rules the element of space

II) Quality of Signs

a) Cardinal sign (Movable or Chara): Aries, Cancer, Libra and Capricorn (1,4,7,10)

Features: Dynamic, Restless, Passionate, Creative, Out-of-the-box thinker, Self-Motivated and Enterprising

b) Fixed Sign (Sthira): Taurus, Leo, Scorpio and Aquarius (2,5,8,11)

Features: Tough, Determined, Loyal, Perfectionists, Supportive, Stubborn and often resist to change

c) Mutable sign (Common or Dual): Gemini, Virgo, Sagittarius and Pisces (3,6,9,12)

Features: Adaptable, Flexible, Observers, Never miss any detail, Open-minded, Unpredictable and Deceptive

III) Masculine & Feminine Signs

a) The masculine signs are Aries, Gemini, Leo, Libra, Sagittarius, and Aquarius.

b) The Feminine signs are Taurus, Cancer, Virgo, Scorpio, Capricorn, and Pisces.

IV) Odd and Even Signs

a) **Odd Signs:** 1,3,5,7,9,11

If there are more planets in odd signs, then the person, despite being a female, is more masculine in appearance and in nature and possesses the qualities of a male. These signs are also called fierce or cruel signs.

b) **Even Signs:** 2,4,6,8,10,12

If there are more planets in these signs, then the person, despite being a male, is more feminine in appearance and in nature and possesses the qualities of a female. These signs are also called auspicious or gentle signs.

V) Sheershodaya & Prishtodaya Signs

a) Sheershodaya Signs – Gemini, Leo, Virgo, Libra, Scorpio and Aquarius – Rise by their head forward

b) Prishtodaya Signs – Aries, Taurus, Cancer, Sagittarius, Capricorn - Rise with their hinder parts

c) Ubhayodaya Signs – Pisces

VI) Diurnal and Nocturnal Signs

a) Diurnal Signs: Leo, Virgo, Libra, and Aquarius

b) Nocturnal Signs: Aries, Taurus, Gemini, Cancer, Sagittarius, and Capricorn

Pisces is strong during twilight.

Due to the rotation of the Earth, half of its side is facing Sun while the other half is away from the Sun at any given time. So, half the Earth has day while the other half has night. Therefore, half the sign is called a diurnal sign and has Sun-like qualities such as; active, creative, etc., and another half the sign has Moon-like qualities as; passive, receptive, etc.

VII) Direction of the Signs

- East - Aries, Leo, Sagittarius

- South - Taurus, Virgo, Capricorn

- West - Gemini, Libra, Aquarius

- North - Cancer, Scorpio, Pisces

VIII) Colour

Aries -Red; Taurus - White; Gemini - Green; Cancer - Rosy or Pink; Leo – Pale-White; Virgo -Variegated or Piebald; Libra - Black; Scorpio- Golden; Sagittarius -Yellow; Capricorn - Variegated or Brown; Aquarius - Dark Brown; Pisces - White or Normal Fish

IX) Caste

- Kshatriya Signs (1,5,9): Aries, Leo, Sagittarius

- Vaishya Signs (2,6,10) : Taurus, Virgo, Capricorn

- Shudra Signs (3,7,11) : Gemini, Libra, Aquarius

- Brahmin Signs (4,8,12) : Cancer, Scorpio, Pisces

X) Fruitful, Semi-Fruitful and Barren Signs

- Fruitful signs: Cancer, Scorpio, Pisces

- Semi-fruitful signs: Taurus, Libra, Sagittarius, Capricorn, Aquarius

- Barren signs: Aries, Gemini, Leo, Virgo

XI) Long, Short & Normal Signs

i) Long: Leo, Virgo, Libra, Scorpio

ii) Short: Aries, Taurus, Aquarius

iii) Normal: Gemini, Cancer, Sagittarius, Capricorn, Pisces

Chapter 4

The Twelve Houses

Astrology has divided the entire space into 12 equal sections. These sections are called Houses or Bhavas (in Sanskrit) means – "Birth, coming into existence". Earth is moving on its axis from West to East and due to its rotation, we can see only one part of the sky at a time. The zodiac moves one after the other towards the horizon, changing every two hours and rising again in the east about 24 hours later. Each bhava has its own meaning and the result of each bhava changes continuously due to the transit of celestial bodies.

The planets ruling the sign are called lord or owner of the house and the planet situated on the sign is a tenant of that house. The strength of the ruling planet is important for the optimum functioning of the house, but the final conclusion will be taken only after the consideration of - the owner, the tenant and aspect of other planets. If the house is vacant, it does not mean that it is worthless, rather it means that there is no tenant (planet) and only the owner of the house is responsible for all the matters related to them including aspect of other planets.

The 12 Houses

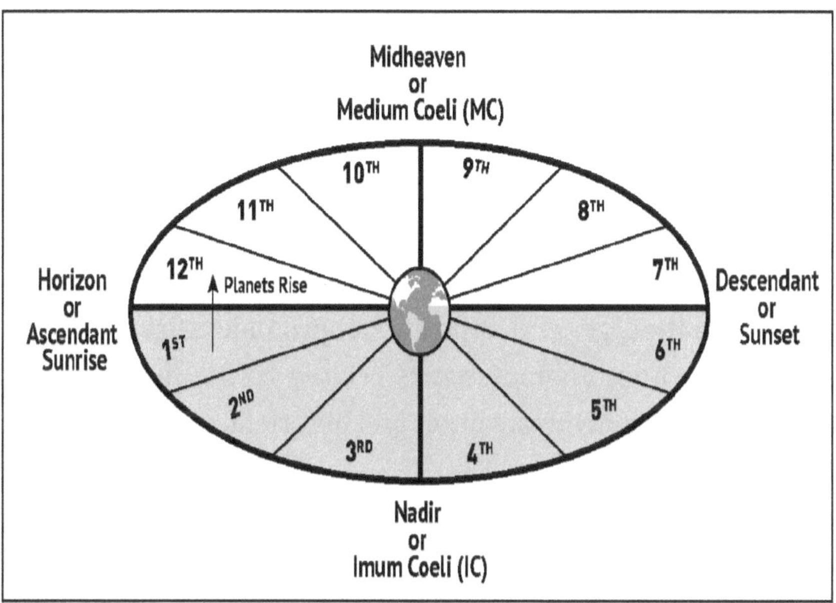

4.1 Meaning of The Twelve Houses

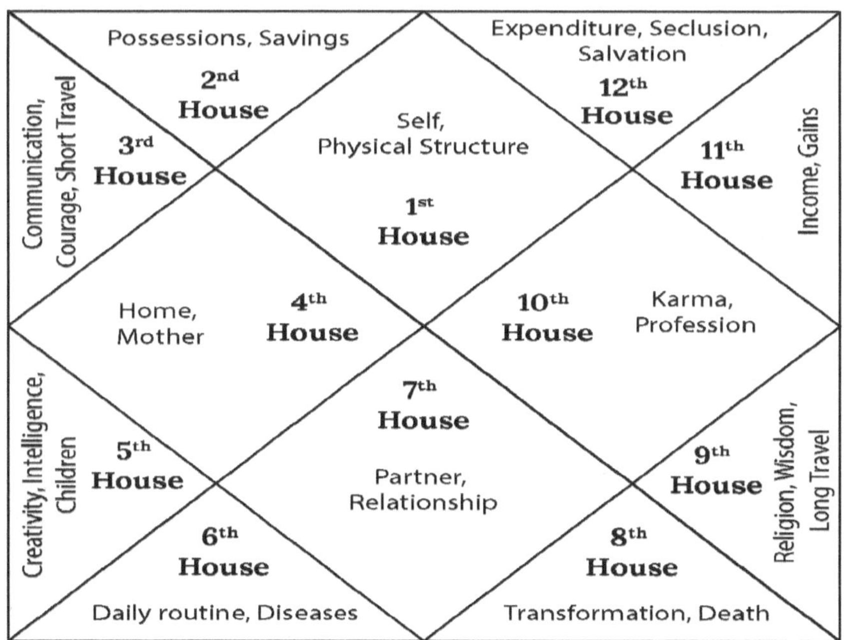

4.1.1 The 1ˢᵗ House

Ascendant is called the first house or bhava of the horoscope, is the sign of the zodiac which is rising on the eastern horizon at the time of birth. The zodiac sign falling on the ascendant and the planets situated on them decide the physical structure of the person. The first house is the house of self. It represents birth, the soul has got a physical body. This physical body contains all the qualities, general appearance, prominent traits, colour, shape, and other characteristics related to the first house. It represents the individual's urges and his orientation towards life in this material world.

This house represents the energy, vitality, general disposition, health, and span of life. If the house is strong, then the person is courageous enough to face any difficulty in life. He is determined and does not waver from difficult circumstances. The first house represents head and brain, name, fame, dignity, self-respect, beauty, prestige, happiness, concern, longevity, etc. When afflicted, weakness and other health-related problems are also seen from here.

4.1.2 The 2ⁿᵈ House

The second house is the house of family, possessions, and savings. The family which we got by birth, i.e., our father, mother, siblings, close relatives, etc. It is the house of wealth and indicates the availability of resources and earning capacity of one. It is important to consider in which house the second lord is situated; the natives are most likely to earn in the profession related to the house.

This house indicates the face and its organs. It indicates eyes – especially the right eye, nose, mouth, nails, and teeth of the native. An afflicted second house indicates vision and speech-related problems. If mercury is afflicted in the 2nd house, the person has a problem of stammering. Jupiter in the 2nd house indicates either a wealthy person or having a large family. Ketu in the second house indicates that the person will have to face serious financial problems for about one and a half years in his life.

This house represents; memory, the quality of oratory and singing, power of observation and imagination, jewellery, precious stones, bonds, securities, stocks and shares, mortgages and other exchangeable assets, food and grains, clothing, second marriage, deception, and unnatural sex, etc.

4.1.3 The 3rd House

This is the house of expression and communication. This house indicates how we develop our language and express ideas toward the world. All types of correspondence, like; letters, papers, documents, etc., and modern means of communication like; mobile phones, email, networking, television, etc. are considered from this house. This is the house of writing, editing, translation, teaching and public speaking. It includes – thinking, understanding, contemplation, gathering facts and reporting in a presentable manner.

This is the house of siblings – especially younger brothers and sisters, cousins, neighbours, casual acquaintances and indicates relationship towards them. This is the house of short journeys, lust, and transportation. This house covers courier services, deliveries, messengers, post offices and comes in handy when dealing with these activities.

This is the house of inspiration and courage, where the third lord is situated, it shows that the person will be motivated to do the matters related to that house. For example, the lord of the third house in the eighth house shows that the person will take interest in the occult science, the lord of the third house in the fifth house shows that the person likes to do work related to his hobbies.

This house represents; the functioning of the mind and power, ear – especially the right ear, arms, wrists, hands, fingers, shoulders, and nervous system. The practice of pranayama and other breathing exercise belongs to this house.

4.1.4 The 4th House

The 4th house relates to the Moon. It represents our emotions, sensitivity, psychology, heart, and happiness. This is the house of the mother and represents our early childhood education. This is the house of our home and family – the family which we create in this world. It represents peace and domestic environment. The atmosphere of the family is good if this house is strong and receives good aspects. This house is also considered a 'Grave' which represents all hidden things and secret affairs of the native.

This house of early education indicates school and college-level education while the 9th house indicates research and higher education. This is the house of the masses and indicates the popularity of the person. Venus in the air sign indicates that the person will be famous in the public sphere. Moon located in the fourth house gives the person the pleasure of living in his own beautiful house. This house indicates vehicles and conveyances, houses, movable and immovable property, leased or rented property, real estate, land, comforts, and luxuries.

An afflicted 4th house indicates; physical ailments of the breast and chest, mental disorder, problems in the lungs, lunacy, and problem related to the circulatory system. It is the most sensitive house and afflictions indicate a lack of peace. Where the lord of the fourth house is situated, the person will seek happiness in the matter related to that house.

The 4th house is the lowest point of the zodiac, which is called Nadir point or IC (Imum Coeli). The 4th house expresses the inner self of the individual and it is opposite the 10th house which is called Midheaven or MC (Medium Coeli). When Saturn transit through Nadir point, the time is good for meditation and learning esoteric science and when it transits through Midheaven, the native draws a lot of attention to the public persona.

4.1.5 The 5ᵗʰ House

This is the house of our creativity which takes place at different levels of manifestation. It is the house of the fruits of our efforts that manifest in time. The relation of the fifth house with the Kendra houses is very auspicious and provides good results. This is the house of our children – creativity manifests on the physical plane. Moisture is required for conception, so a water sign in the 5th house is good for procreation, while a barren sign indicates trouble and requires medical treatment; however, other factors need to be considered in the chart. This is the house of love affairs and the planets in this house indicate how we show our love to others.

This is the house of worship, religion, wisdom, intelligence, knowledge, mantras, and intuition. This house is known as "Poorva Punya Sthana" i.e., good deeds from our previous birth.

All our hobbies and creativities are nothing but the accumulation of all our deeds. When we pour some water on the surface, it dries up after some time, but when we pour water again, it follows the same path where the water disappeared earlier. In this way our "Karma i.e., Deeds" compels us to act in this material world, which the 5th house represents. This house signifies our desire to fulfill our destiny, by developing our creativity.

This house belongs to our abdomen, entertainment, sports, speculation, gambling, creative arts, traditional laws, ancient literature, advisory, change in job and profession, learning, and teaching. The location of the 5th lord indicates that the native likes to work on matters related to that house. Jupiter in the 5th house gives auspicious results and shows the wise, generous and kind nature of the person.

4.1.6 The 6th House

It is the house of our immunity, disease, struggle, and competition. The immune system protects our body from outside invaders. Therefore, it is necessary to have a strong sixth house for good health. If his 6th house is strong and enjoys beneficial aspects, the person will be able to overcome all the resistances and obstacles in life and will never be disappointed in matters related to health, competition, work, etc. The malefic planet in the 6th house indicates disease, resistance, and obstructions. It is the house of injury and signifies wounds and accidents. This house is related to dietary habits and food. Planets placed here indicate peculiarities in eating habits.

This is the house of our daily work, routine, and service. It rules schedules, organization, fitness, competitors, and enemies. It relates to worry and annoyance. This house belongs to our subordinates and servants. A strong 6th house indicates the person will overpower his enemies and will keep under control his subordinates. The faithfulness of juniors is also ascertained from this house, they will listen, respect, and obey the master if benefic planets are posited or aspected here.

6th house belongs to; pet animals, domestic creatures, tenants, hygiene, cleanliness, maternal uncle, disputes, miseries, litigation, debt, pickpocketing, the danger of snakebite, prison-life. Body parts - waist, navel, lower abdomen, and small intestine. This is the house of discipline; placement of the 6th lord indicates in which area of our life we require discipline.

4.1.7 The 7th House

From 1st house to 6th house represents our individuality, till here the soul is individual, but now it is looking for a partner whose 7th house represents. The soul is fed up with being alone, and now looking for relationships and encounters getting various experiences. The 7th house to the 12th house represents the outer world. The 7th house denotes marriage and partnership.

A strong house represents a long-term relationship between partners but if afflicted and occupied by malefic planets, then the person is not a trustworthy person and has many sexual relations. The timing of marriage is also seen from this house and delay or denial in marriage is possible if it is afflicted and does not receive any beneficial aspect.

All relationships, including business relationships and expressions of physical urge, belong to this house. A person's relationship with others tells him about his social nature and the environment around him. This house indicates how one chooses to present oneself to the outside world, like; wearing beautiful clothes, drinks, perfumes, flowers, etc. This house represents; war, victory over the enemy, rewards, business contracts and agreements, sexual and urinary diseases, etc.

At the higher level, it is the house of Divine Partnership. The ultimate result of the search for a partner is divine search, the drink the soul is seeking is divine nectar, the perfume it seeks is divine fragrance, and victory over the enemy is victory over human weaknesses. That's why the lovers say among themselves – "I see God in you". In India, in a symbolic way husband is called 'Pati Parmeshwar', the soul has met his partner – "The Divine Partner". The search for a partner starts from the seventh house and will continue till the soul meets its "Divine Companion".

4.1.8 The 8th House

This house signifies all hidden things in our lives; Serious and unknown diseases, unexpected wealth, lottery, unknown mental sufferings, difficulties, and transformation. This house is considered for both longevity and death. This is the house of 'Kundalini Shakti' where the serpent power is sleeping and waiting for awakening. This house represents our partner's wealth, inheritance, and wealth from legacies.

A strong house indicates research, philosophical mind, knowledge of the occult and hidden science, investigation power, and nature of spy. The person is able to do deep research and find out the truth from the abyss.

If the house is afflicted then it indicates ignorance and lack of knowledge, the person belongs to the underworld, does not hesitate to do evil deeds, is of a criminal mind, a druggist, a prostitute, a manipulative person, etc.

This is the house of; vulnerability, fear, scandal, accident, insurance, pension and gratuity, retirement, theft, robbery, loans, bankruptcy, divorce, misfortunes, depression, and disappointment. Body parts represented by the house are - sexual organs, scrotum, anus, pelvic bones, etc.

Saturn in the 8th house indicates the long life of the person and prevents any mishappening.

4.1.9 The 9th House

This is the house of father, dharma, religion and luck. Jupiter is the significator of the house and represents knowledge, religion, faith, optimism, worship, and penance. This is the house of our fortune, the house of the fruits of the actions of our past lives. The placement or aspect of Jupiter on this house represents good fortune and the person is religious and kind in nature. Saturn in the ninth house indicates that the person will take interest in meditation and other spiritual activities, but the affliction to the house points to a fanatical person who does not hesitate to commit any offense on a matter related to the religion.

The 9th house represents; long journeys, higher knowledge and education, experts, advisors, gurus, visit to holy places, philosophy, law, courts, temples, medicine, remedies, etc.

This house represents inquisitiveness, discovery and exploration. Jupiter and fire sign indicate wisdom and such a person has to transcend domestic boundaries to gain insight. This house covers foreign affairs and cross-cultural relations, international travel and matter related with it like passport, visas, etc. This house signifies the sharing of knowledge and expertise. Hence, this house is associated with printing, publishing and broadcasting.

Body parts represented by the house are – thighs and hips. Weakness of this house indicates trouble in thighs, leukemia, diabetes, etc. This house presides over; invention, discovery, and exploration.

4.1.10 The 10th House

When Sun is at its highest point it is known as Midheaven or Medium Coeli (MC) and in a horoscope, the 10th house represents this point. The Sun touches the mid-sky point every day at noon, so it is at the highest angle of heaven. This is the house of our karma and represents the career and social status of the person. A strong 10th house is necessary for a successful career in life. The placement of the 10th lord indicates the nature of the profession of the person. This is the house of rules and commands. A strong Sun indicates high organizational capability and a government job.

This house is directly above the earth at one's birth. It is opposite the Nadir Point or IC which is represented by the 4th house. Hence, actions and anomalies associated with the house are highly visible. The transit of Saturn through this house indicates the high worldly activities of the native. To determine one's career 2nd, 6th and 10th house should be analyzed carefully because these are earthy signs and represents material gains.

This house represents; profession, source of livelihood, nature of work, reputation, promotion, public image, ambition, glory, fame, government service, political power, employer, superior, proficiency in a profession, etc. Weakness in the 10th house indicates a problem related to the profession. When any malefic planet transits over the 10th house problem related to the profession are incurred.

Body parts – knee and kneecaps, joints, and bones. An afflicted house indicates broken knees, arthritis, inflammation of joints, etc. The knee supports the movement of the body, it is very flexible, delicate, and complex. It has the ability to handle pressure and without it, we cannot stretch our bodies. One wrong move can throw the entire structure in disarray. Similarly, the planet and its lord in the tenth house are of great importance. One wrong move related to them can disturb the whole career.

This house tells about our ability to handle work pressure. The planets and lords of the tenth house indicate our ability to handle situations at work and our obligation to perform our duties. A strong tenth house indicates that the person will not be disappointed in the adverse circumstances related to the profession and will perform his duties responsibly.

4.1.11 The 11th House

This is the house of income, gains, and fulfillment of desires. This is the house of our hopes, wishes, and aspirations. It represents our friendship, social lives, success in endeavors, recovery of lost money, and satisfaction of personal needs. This house represents attachment, affection, and excessive indulgence for material gain. Malefics in the house indicate a native can be passionately attached to his desire and go to any extreme to fulfill it.

Houses 1 to 10 represent our various sources of gains and the 12th house is the house of expenditure. When we add all gains and deduct expenses, the remainder is called the net balance, which represents the 11th house. This is the house of counseling and sharing. The 5th house indicates our hobbies, 11th house represents the playground for those hobbies.

This house represents; originality, eccentricity, insights, all future-oriented things, astronomy, modern technology, electronic media, networking, elder siblings, son's wife, friends, social activities, cooperation, honor in public functions, extra-marital relationships, recovery from illness, foreign collaboration, litigation, etc. Body parts - left ear, ankles, shanks, shin bone, etc. A weak house represents pain, fracture, and wounds in these parts.

4.1.12 The 12th House

It is the house of moksha (spiritual liberation), solitude, meditation, and monastery. It is the house of self-sacrifice and selfless deeds. Saturn or its aspect in the twelfth house indicates that the person will go into deep mediation and leave the rest of his life in isolation or in a monastery.

This house represents the secret working of the human mind. Therefore, this house indicates conspiracy, cunningness, fraud, deception, envy, malice, etc. It represents bedroom, sleep, and sexual pleasures. The 7th house shows our partner but the 12th house shows indulgence and experience in sex. A weak house indicates anxiety, sleep disturbance, and quarrels in the bedroom. It is a house of exile and imprisonment.

This house represents; foreign land, obstructions in life, seclusion, hospitalization, asylum, suicide, secret opponent, sexually transmitted disease, loss of a spouse, termination of employment, misfortune, etc. Body parts – left eye, feet. An affliction to the 12th house or its lord indicates a problem in the left eye or in feet. An afflicted house can put the person into seclusion either in prison or in hospitalization.

The sixth house indicates borrowing and the twelfth house indicates loan repayment. To get rid of debt, the twelfth house and its owner should be studied carefully. It is the house of loss and expenditure. Jupiter in the twelfth house signifies that the person will be protected by Jupiter for any loss in life, including threats to life. But the planet of expansion in the expenditure house shows that the person is extravagant and unable to control his expenses.

The third house represents immediate desire, while the 12th house represents the deeper subconscious mind, imagination, intuition, and spirituality. In other words, the 12th house represents the destination, while the third house represents the efforts to get there. Dreams are denoted by the 12th house, and the fulfillment of dreams is done by the 3rd house.

4.2 Types and Classifications of Houses

The 12 houses or bhavas are classified in several groups:

4.2.1 Dharma, Artha, Kama, Moksha Houses

a) The Dharma Houses

Houses 1st, 5th, and 9th are called the houses of Dharma (Righteousness/Duty). The firehouse triplicity represents a sense of duty and mission in this life. They are considered auspicious houses and the planets in these signs represent the fulfillment of dharma or duty. These are the houses of purity, truth, and integrity. Fire signs represent the pursuit of knowledge.

The first house represents the direction of life and dharma for oneself. The 5th house represents dharma for children, intelligence, talents, and skills. Being a house of dharma, one should not misuse his talent for personal gain. The position or aspect of Saturn on this house indicates that if a person misuses his talent, he will get severe punishment. The ninth house represents dharma for our father, our religion, etc. Wherever the lord of these houses is situated, it indicates that the person has to fulfill his duty related to the respective houses.

b) The Artha Houses

Houses 2, 6, and 10 are the Artha houses (Prosperity/Wealth). Artha means materials and possessions, therefore, these house deals with our resources. Planets posited here and the placement of their lords indicates how we get it and can manage it. The second house deals with wealth, the person will face scarcity of money, if a debilitated planet is situated here, an exalted planet indicates an abundance of resources. The 6th house indicates how we organize our daily work. The person will face a struggle in his daily life if the 6th house is not supported by benefic planets. The 10th house indicates our career and social status. This is the peak point of the horoscope and represents all our efforts to fulfill our material needs.

c) The Kama Houses

Every person has a desire, but what type of desire is there, the 3rd, 7th, and 11th houses indicate those urges, which are called Kama Houses (Pleasure/Desire). The third house represents our ambition and courage to venture into new areas. The seventh house represents the desire for relationships; relationship with spouse, relationship in business, and with the outside world. The 11th house indicates the desire for wealth and the position of its owner indicates the path to attain it. It also indicates the desire for friends and social activities.

d) The Moksha Houses

The 4th, 8th and 12th houses are Moksha (Liberation/Salvation) houses. These water houses have the power to liberate the soul. As water dissolves everything, similarly these houses have the ability to remove every weakness of human beings and give salvation to the soul. 4th house indicates peace and pleasure, the 8th house indicates quest for an unknown spiritual world and the 12th house indicates solitude, meditation, and renunciation. The planets placed here and the lord of the houses shows the path to achieve this.

4.2.2 The Kendra Houses

The 1st, 4th, 7th, and 10th houses are known as Kendra houses. It is considered to be a strong and positive house. These houses provide strength and the planets located in them are considered to be endowed with full manifestation power. These houses have given very much importance in Vedic astrology and the placement of any Kendra lord in a Kendra house or any aspect of the house by its lord provides beneficial results for the native.

4.2.3 The Trikona or Trine Houses

Houses 1, 5, and 9 are known as Trikona houses. These are fortunate houses and bring wisdom and luck. The formation of the triangle of the fire sign houses represents the synergy with each other, the planets located here support each other and make the path easy. In case, the planet located here may not be very favorable, it will only express its bright side and help the person to move forward. A debilitated planet indicates a lack of resources, but the person will work very hard to achieve his goal.

4.2.4 The Upachaya Houses

Houses 3rd, 6th, 10th, and 11th are called Upachaya houses. Upachaya means development and growth. These are the houses of growth as we move forward in life and the planets placed here to increase and improve their results over time. If the lord of a Upachaya house is posited in his own house or another Upachaya house it indicates growth and success over time.

4.2.5 The Dushtana Houses

Houses 6th, 8th, and 12th are considered Dusthana (malefic) houses. The sixth house indicates challenges in our daily life. It is also the house of growth. This indicates that as we progress in our lives, our challenges will also increase. The planets located here indicate the growth of a person as well as new challenges. For example; A person has got promotion in his career, this will increase his social status and income. But the new position has come with new challenges along with relocation, which disturbed his earlier daily life. He found both growth and difficulty together. Hence 6th house is both – a dushtana and upachaya house.

The 8th house is the house of transformation. There is no transformation without suffering and difficulties. The planets and their lords teach tough lessons to a person and force him to change.

What comes after attaining name, fame, wealth, and other material desires. The twelfth house indicates that there is no meaning in wandering around in this material world. It is the house of loss, detachment from the material world, and the planets here will teach all these lessons. Experience is the only teacher in this world whose lessons no one denies.

4.2.6 The Maraka Houses

The 2nd and 7th houses are called the Maraka houses. The 8th house is the house of longevity, but it's a complex house representing death, transformation, inheritance, secrets, and deep psychology. As per Bhavat Bhavam, the 8th to 8th house is the 3rd house which is also considered the house of longevity. The 12th house is the house of loss, and loss of longevity is death. Hence, the 12th from the 8th and 3rd house is the 7th and 2nd house which is called Maraka houses, and the lord of the house is called Marakesh. These houses as considered death-determining houses. However, physical death is an extremely important event and cannot be determined by a single house.

Chapter 5

The Planets

Vedic astrology considers the influence of nine planets in our birth chart. Sun, Moon, Mercury, Venus, Mars, Jupiter, Saturn, and two shadow planets Rahu and Ketu. Each planet represents its own unique characteristics, which affect the physical and mental activities of the individual and the things around him.

The Sun and the Moon are the two luminaries in the sky that are not planets, the other five being planets and can be seen from the Earth. Rahu and Ketu being shadow planets are not visible, but the subtle energy of these two planets affects the life of the person and the conditions of the earth. All Planets aspect 7th house from the position occupied by them. However, Mars, Jupiter, Saturn, and Rahu have special aspects besides the 7th aspect. Ketu has no aspect.

Planets and their Characteristics

5.1 The Sun

The Sun is considered to be the king of the universe. It is a symbol of the soul and the 'Lord of Sunday'. The Sun moves in only one direction, never retrogrades, stay one month in a sign, and completes the entire zodiac in a year. It is the center of the solar system and everything revolves around the Sun.

In India, we worship Surya as the Sun God, who is the supreme giver and everything on this earth originated from the Sun. The Sun is life, without that there is no life on earth. Sun is exalted at 10 degrees in Aries and powerful in the other two fire signs; Leo and Sagittarius. It is debilitated at 10 degrees in Libra and faces difficulties in the other two air signs; Gemini and Aquarius. Its own sign and Mooltrikona sign both is Leo.

Astronomy: The Sun is the centre of the solar system. It is the biggest object and contains 99.8% of the solar system's mass. It is about 150 million kilometres from Earth. Its gravity holds the solar system together. It is not a solid mass; it is composed of layers made up almost entirely of hydrogen and helium. The surface of the Sun is about 10,000 degrees Fahrenheit (5,500 degrees Celsius) hot, while temperatures in the core reach more than 27 million F (15 million C). It has a well-known sunspot cycle which has a maximum of around every 11 years. The Sun is the source of enormous amount of energy, part of which provides the light and heat needed to support life on Earth.

Direction and Digbala: The direction of the Sun is east. It gets directional strength (Digbala) in the 10th house and weakness when it is placed in the 4th house.

Classification: It is a Sattvic planet and controls our consciousness. It is a fiery, dry, and masculine planet. Its colour is red and the caste is Kshatriya. It controls metals - gold, copper, and ruby. It represents coarse clothes and the age of 50 years old. It represents the summer season and organic matter. It represents bones, average height, steadfast tendency, and upward direction. It represents places of worship and temples, mountain trees, and pungent taste like; onion, ginger, black pepper, chilies, etc.

Characteristics: The Sun is 'Self' and 'Esteem'. It provides illumination and warmth. The shining Sun in the sky represents strength, energy, and vitality. It represents the power of resistance. It is bold and forceful. It represents mental strength and confidence. It is ego and pride. It represents father, authority, government, and honor from government, high status, fame, victory, and enlightenment. Strong Sun in the horoscope makes a person determined and decisive. It gives high energy, commanding power, quality of leadership, respect of elders, and good quality of listening.

A strong Sun represents a charismatic personality. The person will be ambitious, energetic, influential, and kind-hearted. The person will be courageous enough to go alone, even in difficult circumstances without any fear. He will not be ready to compromise anything for his dignity and honor. In my corporate career, I have seen that people are ready to quit their jobs but are not ready to compromise on their dignity if the Sun is strong on their chart. They are ready to bear anything in life for their self-respect. In such a situation, worshiping the Sun God daily is beneficial for the person.

Sun gets exalted in Aries, a fiery sign of Mars. Aries represents the solo spirit and does not wait for others to come. Aries means – at the top of the mountain alone. The nature of this sign is suitable for the Sun – King, so, it is exalted here. While Libra is a marketplace, is totally against the tendency of the Sun. Therefore, the Sun gets debilitated in Libra.

Sun controls our eyesight, to regain eye-sight and vitality in life people in India worship Lord Sun. When the sunlight comes everything is visible. In the same way, wherever the Sun is placed in your chart everything will become visible and you cannot hide it.

Affliction: If Sun is afflicted in a chart, then the person will easily become tempered, arrogant, jealous, irritable, dominating, pretentious, lavish, conceit, and haughty. Such people do not listen to anyone's advice and consider themselves supreme. They are not ready to change their ideas/plans under any circumstances and expect others to accept them.

Body parts and diseases: Sun rules our head, brain, eyes, heart, lungs, blood, and circulation. Diseases; blood pressure, eye diseases, fever, cerebral disorders, etc.

5.2 The Moon

The Moon is the earth's only natural satellite. It is considered the queen of the solar system. It moves 13.2 degrees per day, completes one orbit around the earth in 27.3 days, and rises on an average 50 minutes late every day. The half of the Moon which is towards the Sun can be seen from the earth and is called the phases of the Moon.

The cycle of lunar phases takes 29.5 days, known as the synodic period, which is longer than the sidereal period of 27.3 days. The reason for this difference is the Moon returns to the same place in the sky once every sidereal period, but the Sun is also moving in the sky. When the Moon returns to the same place in the sky, the Sun moves 27 degrees. It takes the Moon about two days to catch this difference. Moon's own sign is Cancer, it gets exalted in Taurus at 3 degrees which is also its Mooltrikona sign, it gets debilitated in Scorpio at 3 degrees.

Understanding the different phases of the Moon is very important in astrology. When the Moon is exactly opposite the Sun (180° or 7th house) in a horoscope, it is a full moon day. Moon is considered weak within 72 degrees from the Sun. Amavasya (new moon) occurs when Sun and Moon both are in the same house and less than 13.2 degrees from each other.

Astronomy: The Moon is the only natural satellite of the Earth. Its average distance from Earth is 385,000 km and the Earth rotates on its axis once every 27.3 days (a sidereal month). Its daytime temperature is 225°F (107°C), while night-time temperatures are -243°F (-153°C). It has a solid, rocky surface covered with craters, mountain ranges, rills (long narrow channels), and lava plains.

Direction and Digbala: The direction of the Moon is North-West; it gets directional strength (Digbala) in the 4th house and weakness in the 10th house.

Classification: Moon is a watery planet, represents moist and rainy season and watery places like; well, water tanks, bathrooms, watery surfaces, rivers, bays, ocean, etc. Its color is white and indicates a small height. It represents new fabric and organic matter. It represents salty taste (sea salt, rock salt), gems, spotless pearls, silver, and other white metals. It belongs to the Vaishya caste and represents the age of 70 years old. It represents the coconut tree, fruits, vegetables, and all watery substances.

Characteristics: Moon is a Sattvik planet and controls our minds. It is a feminine planet, represents mother in the chart, peace of mind, and rules our emotions. It represents selflessness like a mother and the tender qualities of a female. It represents the nourishing quality, sensitivity, and imagination of the person. A strong Moon indicates a strong mind, friendly nature, and pleasing personality. The person is receptive, decisive, mature, helpful in nature, and clear in his thoughts. Such a person never wastes time in vain things, wants the discussion to come to the point, and takes no interest in idle gossip.

Being the representative of the mother in the horoscope, the person should always respect his mother and should never quarrel with her, if he wants that his Moon always remains strong.

Moon rules over the masses, the 4th house is the house of the masses, if Moon is situated in the 4th house, then the popularity of the person is indicated. Moon being a feminine planet bestows attractiveness and other feminine qualities. The person under the influence of the Moon as a ruling planet takes interest in taking care of others. It indicates professions related to fluids, doctors, psychologists, therapists, child care, and other nurturing and healing professions.

The Sun represents the father, the moon represents the mother. The Sun represents the seed, the Moon represents the womb.

The Sun represents the order and the Moon represents the fulfillment of the order. The Moon has no light and is always dependent on sunlight. The Sun shows independence and the weak Moon indicates that the person is looking for support and is always afraid of being alone. The Sun represents the present, the Moon represents the past. If Moon is situated in any house from the 9th to 12th house, then the person takes interest in subjects like; History, Archaeology, Astrology, etc. The person memorizes the dates of historical events easily and is quick to learn these subjects.

When the Moon placed less than 72 degrees from the Sun, it indicates less sunlight and due to absence of sunlight the native is prone to diseases easily. Such native must worship lord Sun in his whole life.

The sign of Taurus is highly suitable for the Moon. Taurus is a feminine sign – fertile and receptive, it is a highly fertile land in the zodiac. The nature of Taurus is to produce and grow things. Its symbol is the bull which is known for its sensuality and fertility. Taurus represents luxury and comfort, therefore, the Moon – the Queen, finds this sign perfectly suitable for herself, and becomes exalted at 3 degrees in the sign (Upon entering here, the queen found a very suitable place for her stay). Scorpio is a sign of ruthlessness and represents muddy water which is totally against the nature of the Moon – the Queen, and it gets debilitated in the sign while entering (3 degrees).

Affliction: An afflicted moon indicates a person will become depressed, pessimistic, impulsive, timid and over-anxious, dreamers, self-destructive, insane, and psychic. A weak moon indicates a person can be easily influenced by outside energies and unable to take decisive decisions.

Body parts and diseases: The organs ruled by the Moon are; Blood, saliva, womb, abdomen, and breasts of women. According to medical astrology, surgical operations should be avoided during the full moon as there is more fluid at this time. Diseases; cough and cold, lunacy, paralysis, hysteria, epilepsy, etc.

5.3 Mars

The Red Planet Mars is considered the Commander-in-Chief of the Solar System and denotes strength in the horoscope. According to Hindu mythology, Mars is called Mangal or Bhauma and is believed to be the brother (or son) of Earth. Mars represents energy, either constructive or destructive. It shows our ambition, passion, and desire. Energy should always be controlled as it can lead us to act indiscriminately without thinking or with no direction, and it can create problems. Mars becomes exalted at 28° in Capricorn and debilitated at 28° in Cancer. It rules over Aries and Scorpio, where first it has a positive sign and later it has a negative sign.

Astronomy: Mars, the fourth planet from the Sun, is easily seen in the sky - a bright red dot in the sky. Mars is easiest to observe when it and the Sun are on opposite sides in the sky. Its distance from the Sun is 228 million km. Mars orbits the Sun once in 687 Earth days and completes one revolution every 24.6 hours. Mars has a thin atmosphere composed of carbon dioxide, nitrogen, and argon, its surface is covered by loose dust and rock. Its soil is rich in iron gives its red colour. It has about one-tenth the mass of Earth. Mars has two moons, Phobos and Deimos.

Direction and Digbala: The direction of Mars is South; it gets directional strength (Digbala) in the 10th house and weakness in the 4th house.

Classification: Mars is considered a Tamasic and fiery planet. It is a masculine and Kshatriya caste planet. It is a dry and barren planet and indicates a tense and quarrelsome situation. It represents accidents, fires, disputes, destruction, wars, and sexual drive. Its colour is blood-red and stone is coral. It represents the summer season and fiery places. It deals with burnt clothing and inorganic substances. It represents young age and low height. Its taste is bitter and the tendency is violent. It represents upward movement.

Characteristics: Mars is considered a malefic and ruthless planet. Being the lord of weapons and war, Mars does not think twice. If it is favourable in the horoscope, it bestows good qualities; One will be courageous, will fight evils, and will do heroic deeds. The character of the person is strong, determined, passionate and the person is not afraid of any kind of obstacles in life. He is a great protector and always uses his sword to protect others. He can go to any extent to save someone's life.

Mars represents the drive, courage, initiation, and adventurous nature of the person. It represents determination, confidence, sharp wit, and leadership quality. The position of Mars in the birth chart shows where the physical activity will take place and indicates what kind of things will excite you, how you deal with disputes and react to stressful situations, violence, etc. Mars represents the younger brother, land, and property and rules the animal instincts in man. Mars believes in overcoming obstacles by force rather than any strategy. This indicates the impulsive nature of a person with a quick activity.

Martians are the pioneers and have risk-taking inclinations. It belongs to entrepreneurs, conquerors, adventurers, and athletes. They like to conduct large-scale operations that requires high energy. Mars indicates new ventures and its beneficial aspects indicate the floating of new companies.

As Commander-in-Chief, the most important thing for Mars is to win the battle. Similarly, the most important thing for a quarrelsome person is to win the argument, no matter how. Mars positioned in the sixth house within the Uttara Ashadha Nakshatra indicates an individual of an extremely quarrelsome nature, ready to pick a fight instantly over any issue. For such a person, the subject of the dispute holds no significance; they simply seek out any pretext to initiate a quarrel and remain ever-eager to fight. Therefore, a wise man never indulges in any discussion with such a person. An afflicted Mars indicates that the person can go to any extreme to win the argument and fight. However, such a placement of Mars is not good for married life.

Mars represents action and energy. Action without a goal is a waste of energy. The energy of Mars should be used in a constructive manner and in spiritual activities. Mars gets exalted in Capricorn, a sign of Saturn. Capricorn represents a high level of restrictions and control. In this sign, Martian energy is fully controlled; when energy is fully controlled it produces maximum results. Mars gets exalted at 28 degrees in Capricorn, at this point, Mars energy is fully controlled (However, Saturn treats Mars as its enemy). Cancer, a sign of the Moon has no power to control Martian energy. Therefore, Mars gets debilitated in this sign.

We move into this world due to Martian energy. To burn energy, fuel is required and that fuel is our desire. If the fuel (desire) produces smoke, it not only disturbs the life of the person but also the environment around him. Mars represents fire, and the scar of fire does not go easily. Therefore, one must control Martian energy in a constructive manner so that it should not produce smoke and should not leave a scar.

Mars indicates physical sports and exercise, the iron and steel industry, police department, firefighting department, military activities, etc. It represents fiery places like; the kitchen, engine room, and boilers. It indicates cuts, wounds, scars, strikes, conspiracy, criminals, murderers, thieves, robbers, etc.

Affliction: If the planet is afflicted then the person will use all his power to fulfil his desire and can go to any extent. Irrespective of how many fingers are burnt, the fulfilment of desire is very important for him and if the person is running on the Mahadasha of Mars, then dangerous consequences can be possible, as he is not ready to give up his desire under any circumstances. A weak and afflicted Mars makes the native a sexual pervert.

The afflicted Mars indicates that the native will easily lose his temper and start abusing others without thinking. The person will become quarrelsome and will be ready to fight over trivial matters; Scratches on a car and people are ready to fight on the street. The afflicted Mars does not like differences of opinion with anyone. The native will argue in vain, instead of giving any intelligent argument, he prefers to use force and feels the joy of winning the battle.

Body Parts and diseases: Bone marrow, forehead, nose, urinary system, external sex organs, prostate gland, muscle tissue, etc. Diseases: Bleeding, menstrual disorders, abortion, smallpox, chickenpox, fistula, burns, cuts, wounds, measles, malaria, diseases of the bone marrow, etc.

5.4 Mercury

Mercury is considered as Prince of the solar system and "Messenger to the Gods". As per Hindu mythology, Mercury is a child of the Moon. Mercury rules our intelligence, intellect, memory, reasoning, power of speech, etc. It is a planet of trade and commerce and represents all financial activities. Mercury gets exalted at 15° in Virgo and debilitated at 15° in Pisces. It rules over Gemini and Virgo, where first it has a positive sign and later it has a negative sign.

Astronomy: Mercury is the smallest planet in the solar system and nearest to the Sun. It does not go beyond 28° from the Sun. Mercury is only 1.4 times larger than Moon and it is only visible in the sky at the time of sunrise and sunset. It takes 88 Earth days to complete a single orbit around the Sun. Because the planet is so close to the Sun, its surface temperatures are both extremely hot and cold. The day temperatures can reach highs of 430°C and at night temperatures can dip as low as -180°C. Mercury is not the hottest planet, it is Venus because of its dense atmosphere.

Direction and Digbala: The direction of Mercury is North; it gets directional strength (Digbala) in the 1st house and weakness in the 7th house.

Classification: Mercury is a rajasic planet, its colour is green, and the stone is emerald. It is considered a boy and represents playgrounds and living beings. Its metal is alloy and the gender is eunuch. It belongs to the Vaishya caste and represents wet clothes. It represents mixed tastes and a mixture of diverse qualities. It represents skin, short in height, and sideways momentum. It represents wet crop, brinjal, ladyfinger, beetroot, etc. It belongs to the Sharad season (from 20 Sept. to 19 Nov. approx.).

Characteristics: Mercury is considered to be a child and children have a tendency to imitate elders, similarly, Mercury reflects the characteristics of the planet with which it is associated. Children must be nurtured by their parents and elders. Similarly, Mercury must be associated with benefics. Mercury alone in a house or its association with malefics does not produce good results.

Mercury indicates how we express ourselves to the outside world. It indicates literary pursuit and makes a person good at speaking, learning, proficient in many languages, and orator. It represents analytical ability, planning, diplomacy, accounting, ideas, thoughts, talkative person, jokes, intelligence, writing, editing, publishing, etc. It indicates colleges, schools, shops, and market place.

Mercury creates a sharp mind, awareness, deep research, and mystery seekers. Strong mercury is required to be good at maths and astrology. It indicates that the person will be able to grasp the subject quickly, have good retentive power, and will be strong in mental calculations. Mercury indicates connections, many friends, correspondence, news, and information.

Mercury is mutable and represents restlessness nature and lack of consistency. Therefore, Mercurians must learn stability and perseverance in their lives. The placement of mercury in a chart indicates an inquisitive and curious person. It shows the dexterity, ingenuity, and versatile nature of the person. However, if the person possesses a firm and steady attitude and leaves his restless then he will perform better in his work. Because Mercury's nature is mutable, it indicates that if a person involves themselves in overindulgence in a work, then he will leave it after some time.

Mercury's exaltation sign is Virgo – a Mooltrikona sign of Mercury. The sign of Virgo represents virginity and celibacy. Mercury is considered an adolescent as it is yet to attain maturity. Mercury exalted in Virgo indicates that a teenager should follow the path of celibacy to make his mind sharp. Pisces represents sexual pleasure, if a teenager indulges in sexual activities, his Mercury will be debilitated and he will lose courage and ability to speak when needed. Indulgence in sexual activity will also hamper the development of his mind. Such a person will not get a sharp mind in his life; he will remain a person of a very mediocre mind and will never be able to become an intelligent and wise person.

Mercury represents mixed flavour; hence, Mercurians find pleasure in variety. Poor mercury indicates lack of concentration, changing moods, and poor memory. Mercury in the 6th house indicates that the native may have a problem with forgetting. Mercury in the 4th house indicates the person will have to live in many houses.

Affliction: Mercury is the lord of green colour, if it is afflicted then gradually the green colour will disappear from the native's life. Afflicted mercury indicates native will be cunning, liar, eccentric, scandalous, cheater, argumentative, unprincipled, and boastful. It shows the person may be gullible or will cheat his clients and run away with their money.

Body Parts and diseases: Mercury represents the brain, vein, skin, tongue, nervous system, thyroid gland, neck, etc. Diseases:

loss of memory, skin diseases, dumbness, stammering, nervous system disorder, whimsical, giddiness, impotency, insomnia, etc.

5.5 Jupiter

Jupiter is known as the Prime minister in the planetary cabinet and is considered as Dev Guru. It is a fruitful and a "Highly Benefic" planet in astrology. It represents optimism, aspiration, knowledge, and wisdom. The planet of abundance is noble and benevolent. It provides dignity, reputation, and expansion. It rules over finance and family and represents an honest and sincere person. It represents administration and economic activity and rules over law and religion. It is called "The planet of Fortune". Jupiter gets exalted at 5° in Cancer and debilitated at 5° in Capricorn. It rules over Sagittarius and Pisces, where first it has a positive sign and later it has a negative sign.

Astronomy: Jupiter is the largest planet in the solar system, it is more than twice as massive as all the other planets combined. Jupiter's immense volume could hold more than 1,300 Earths. Jupiter has 79 known moons, one year on Jupiter is the same as 11.8 Earth years. Jupiter is a gas giant and doesn't have a solid surface. It has big storms like the Great Red Spot, that's about twice the size of Earth and has raged for over a century.

Direction and Digbala: The direction of Jupiter is North–East; it gets directional strength (Digbala) in the 1st house and weakness in the 7th house.

Classification: Jupiter is considered a watery and sattvic planet. It is a masculine, Brahmin caste planet and represents ether. It indicates treasury, storeroom, and places where money and jewels are deposited. Its colour is yellow, the stone is yellow sapphire, topaz and metal is gold.

It represents a gentle tendency and sweet taste. It represents fat constituents and tall height. It deals with medium clothes, living beings, and age of 30 years old. It indicates Hemant season (20th Nov. to 19th Jan. approx.) and evenly momentum.

Characteristics: Jupiter is considered to be the master. It represents the generosity of the person. Being Dev Guru, one should always respect Jupiter. In the same manner, the person having strong Jupiter attracts respect from others. Jupiter is considered a counsellor and represents all counselling activities.

Jupiter provides wisdom and removes ignorance and darkness. A strong Jupiter indicates a very honest person. He is dutiful and respects law and religion. He is a magnanimous and broad-minded person and does not believe in any type of fighting and works on making the atmosphere congenial. He believes in co-operation, works on a strategy, and waits for the outcome patiently.

Jupiter provides education, interest in religion, spiritual rhymes, philosophy, astrology, and law. A strong Jupiter indicates concentration, mediation, reading habits, thrust for knowledge, benevolence, prudent behaviour, ethics, morals, etc. Jupiter represents abundance, when it is favourable; opportunity knocks on your door. A person having strong Jupiter in his chart never breaches anyone's trust. The person will always show respect to others, favour doing the right things, and follow the path of justice.

Jupiter always prevents the native from difficulties as long as the native follow the righteous path in his life. The person will be protected at the last moment in a state of difficulty when every possible hope is over.

Like a guru teaches lessons to his students and provides his guidance and protection as long as the student follows the guru's advice, but when the student stops listening to the guru after several warnings, the guru simply removes his protective shield. This is the way Jupiter works.

Jupiter punishes the person but not like Mars. Mars's attack is direct and sharp but Jupiter simply goes away without saying anything. When Jupiter becomes malefic, he removes his shield and stops giving direction. Without direction, the person wanders here and there and wastes his time and energy. Due to the absence of Jupiter, the direction fades away from the person's life and his futile wandering starts without any result. The darkness of ignorance gradually submerges the person.

Jupiter represents growth, and the freshwater of Cancer represents life as well as growth. Therefore, Jupiter feels most comfortable in the sign of Cancer and gets exalted here. Cancer is the fourth sign of the zodiac which is ruled by the Moon. The fourth house also represents the mother's womb. A pregnant woman is the best example of Jupiter exalted in Cancer. The unborn baby (fetus) growing in the womb floats in the fluid, indicating life expands in the water.

Swami Vivekananda said, "Strength is Life, Weakness is Death. Expansion is Life, Contraction is Death. Love is Life, Hatred is Death". Jupiter represents all the positive qualities said in the quote. Jupiter represents a person who fulfils his promises and never breaches anyone's trust if a person does against this then Jupiter removes its shield of protection. Jupiter gets debilitated in Capricorn; a sign ruled by Saturn. Capricorn is a sign of a high level of control, restrictions, and limitations. A planet of expansion – Jupiter, feels completely hapless in this sign.

A debilitated Jupiter in a chart indicates that a person wants to do various things in his life, but has to face a problem of lack of resources. He will complete the task only by moving inch by inch.

Jupiter rules our big plans and bestows us, children. When a couple has a child, various necessities of the child start and they take interest in the fulfillment of all these activities, representing the expansion of life in this mundane world. Children are our future; therefore, Jupiter represents the future.

Jupiter is our luck; therefore, people say when someone is going to do an act when the outcome is unknown "Best of Luck", seeking blessings of Lord Jupiter. Jupiter represents the person who follows principles and does not deviate from the chosen path. Materialistic desire does not allure the person, he prefers to face any situation in life but does not ready to surrender his respect.

Jupiter represents; schools and colleges, law-court, temples, places of sermons, legislative assembly, charitable institutions, bank buildings, hospitals, asylums, and all fatty and sweet products. Jupiter represents the husband in the female horoscope. If a native is running from Jupiter Mahadasha or in transit affected by Jupiter, the native has the inclination to eat more sweets than his normal eating.

Physicians write "Rx" at the top of the prescription before writing their medical advice and seek the blessings of Jupiter. Rx is the Latin symbol for the planet Jupiter. Medical astrology states that taking medicine in Jupiter Hora is more beneficial than at any other time.

In which house Jupiter is situated represents an expansion on matters related to the house. Jupiter's placement in a chart indicates a person will adopt ethical principles and take interest in the expansion of activities related to the house concerned. It also indicates our luck resides there.

Affliction: The afflicted Jupiter makes the person extreme and fanatic. It puts the person in the ocean of darkness and in the absence of knowledge, the person is not ready to listen to anyone. Because of his arrogant nature, he wanders here and there without any fruit. Afflicted Jupiter indicates false optimism, false faith, and orthodox beliefs. A weak Jupiter indicates a lack of hope, absence of knowledge, greed, materialistic nature, extravagant, overconfident, lazy, worthless promises, etc.

The native will not be a liberal person; instead of dutiful he will be careless. Show false reputation to others, shying away from religious activities, and chanting spiritual rhymes are very difficult for him. He will always do improper judgments and make mistakes in calculations.

Body Parts and diseases: Jupiter represents the liver, circulation of blood in the arteries, pancreas, hips, and thighs fat in the body. Diseases: Problem in liver, flatulence, jaundice, diabetes, eczema, hernia, etc.

5.6 Venus

Venus is considered a Demon Guru. According to Hindu mythology, the demon Guru has only one eye. Venus is said to be Mahalakshmi, the wife of Lord Vishnu. It is considered the goddess of love. It bestows marriage, beauty, and grace to the person. It offers luxury and comfort. Venus is exalted at 27° in Pisces and debilitated at 27° in Virgo. It rules over Taurus and Libra, where first it has a negative sign and later it has a positive sign.

Astronomy: Venus is the hottest planet in the Solar System and is much closer to the Sun than Earth. It has a dense atmosphere filled with clouds composed of the greenhouse gas carbon dioxide and sulfuric acid. The gas traps heat and keeps Venus warm. Earth is just a little bit bigger than the size of Venus. Venus is unusual because it spins on its axis from east to west i.e., it moves in the opposite direction of Earth and most other planets. It takes about 243 Earth days to spin around just once. It does not go beyond 48° from the Sun. Venus sets after Sunset and rises before the Sun rises. Venus orbits the Sun once every seven and a half months (224.7 days). On Venus, the Sun rises every 117 Earth days, which means the Sun rises two times each year on Venus. Venus is an evening star for about nine months until it passes behind the Sun, then a morning star for nine months as it moves between the Sun and Earth.

Direction and Digbala: The direction of Venus is South-East; it gets directional strength (Digbala) in the 4th house.

Classification: Venus is considered a warm and rajasic planet. It is a feminine, Brahmin caste planet and represents fresh water. Its colour is variegated and represents diamonds and pearls. It represents excellent cloth and bedrooms. Its taste is sour and the tendency is light. It rules over all exotic vegetables, potatoes, cabbages, fruit trees, flower trees, creeping plants, and organic matter. It represents the average height and age of 16 years old. It indicates Vasant season and sideways momentum.

Characteristics: Venus represents a charming personality. People under its influence are kind and sociable. It rules over marriage and represents the wife in the male horoscope. It rules over all kinds of beauty, pleasures, and luxuries of life. It makes a person generous and cheerful. They are soft-spoken and rarely show their anger on their face, when they are angry, they try to remain silent.

Being a feminine planet, Venus represents the qualities of delicacy, nurturing, supportiveness, and creativity. They are gentle people and show graceful manners, they avoid quarrels and turmoil at any cost, and try to lead a happy and peaceful life. They are caring by nature and take care of every member of the family. These people like to live in harmony with everyone. The person always prefers cleanliness in matters related to the house in which Venus is placed in the native's horoscope. For example, if Venus is in the Ascendant, then the person will take care of his clothes and like to eat quality food, such a person never accepts anything degraded.

Venus represents love and love demands attention. The relationship will dry and come to an end if you do not properly feed the relationship. In the same way, in which house Venus is placed, the activities related to the house require your attention. A favorable Venus indicates a good relationship with partners, easy negotiations, and a win-win situation.

Venus is tender and polite. It rules our senses and indicates laziness in a person. Under its influence, a person has a soft body and avoids doing laborious work. Such people like to relax all day, listen to music and avoid doing any productive work. Due to their strong senses, they can catch the subtle vibrations and like singing and dancing. Venus must be strong in a chart to make a good career in art and music, it gives a melodious and pleasing voice to the person.

Venus rules the semen and sexual energy of the human body. Through purification in the human body, blood is converted into sperm, and when a sperm is fertilized it turns into a newborn baby. Therefore, Venus is associated with diamonds. Just as a diamond attracts attention, a newborn baby attracts everyone's attention.

In every purification only the best moves forward, and the waste is removed. Whatever activity the purification process takes place in, it is controlled by Venus. Therefore, Venus represents the best and Saturn represents the waste. For the seeker of truth, the whole world becomes waste, therefore Saturn represents renunciation.

Venus indicates garnishing and has a special influence on clothing and adornments. It indicates makeup, fragrance, delicious food and luxury in life. If we analyze all these things in a subtle way, we know that all these things come through a process of refining, where the final product is tested many times. This is similar to the process of nature making diamonds from coal. Coal undergoes a difficult process of refining by withstanding pressure and heat for millions of years and becomes a diamond.

The outcome provided by Venus take time, everything that shines in life is controlled by Venus and the process of shining always takes time. Hence the place of diamond is forehead. It signifies the transformation of sexual energy into spiritual energy, which moves upwards and reaches the head.

Venus is the lord of Bharani, Purva Phalguni, and Purvashada nakshatras. These three nakshatras are located between Aries, Leo and Sagittarius. It shows that Venusian energy never takes initiative and prefers to wait. A woman prefers to wait than taking initiative. This is also revealed by its gemstone diamond, as it takes a lot of time to form but the result is beyond imagination. That is why every person wants Venus in their life.

Venus is exalted in the twelfth house and it is the house of salvation. The rotation of Venus in the opposite direction of Earth indicates the transformation of sexual energy into spiritual energy, it shows that when the sexual energy moves against the gravitational force of Earth i.e., upward, and reaches the Sahasrara Chakra (Crown Chakra), one will become enlightened. This is the reason why Venus is exalted in the house of Jupiter (the 12th house is the house of Jupiter and Jupiter considers Venus as its enemy). The debilitation of Venus in the 6th house indicates wastage of sexual energy.

Venus represents; Cinema Hall, dancing room, bedroom, banquet, textiles, automobiles, cars, ships, airplanes, glass industry, confectionery, perfume, embroidery, milk, paint, sandal, soar fruits, jewellery, dress, vehicle, sexual pleasure, flowers, drinking water, hotels, honour, respect, female boss, business relation with females, catering, toys, delicious food, juice, drinks, etc.

Affliction: An afflicted Venus indicates over-Indulgence in sexual activities, loss of a partner, separation from the beloved, excessive marriages, loss of prestige, scandals, fond of fancy food and overeating, company of bad friends, etc. A weak Venus indicates that such a person is deeply indulged in drinking alcohol, likes to enjoy his senses and is always in search of some frivolous pleasure.

An afflicted Venus denies the marriage, it indicates quarrels with the partner or a breakup in the relationship. The person will lead an immoral life, obsessed with desires, jealous, and vengeful. Accidents through animals and birds are also indicated by afflicted Venus.

Body Parts and diseases: Eyes, Reproductive organ, Semen, Kidney. Diseases: Problem in eyes, Ovaries, Hysteria, Eczema, Leprosy, Leukoderma, etc.

5.7 Saturn

As per Hindu astrology, Saturn is the son of the Sun. It is called "Yama" and chief governor for longevity and death. Saturn gets exalted at 20° in Libra and debilitated at 20° in Aries. It rules over Capricorn and Aquarius, where first it has a negative sign and later it has a positive sign.

Astronomy: Saturn is the sixth planet from the Sun and the second-largest planet in our solar system. It is a gas giant composed mainly of gases and liquid. It has beautiful rings which are made of pieces of ice, dust, and rock. It is the farthest planet from Earth that is visible to the naked human eye. Saturn completes one revolution of the Sun in 29.5 Earth years.

Direction and Digbala: The direction of Saturn is West; it gets directional strength (Digbala) in the 7th house and weakness in the 1st house.

Classification: Saturn is an airy, dry, cold, and tamasic planet. It is a shudra caste planet and its gender is neutral. Its colour is blue, the metal is iron and lead, and the stone is sapphire. It represents rags, torn clothes, and inorganic matter. It governs the muscles, indicates a tall person, and is related to old age. Its taste is astringent and the tendency is hard. It belongs to thorny and poisonous trees, broom, bitter gourd, onion, drumstick, betel leaves, tobacco, and greens. Its season is Sisira (January–March) and the momentum is downward.

Characteristics: Saturn is a very powerful planet and its effect on life is subtle and more than any other planet, but its effect is very slow and not easily visible. Only those who have the quality of patience can see the effect of Saturn. It controls our muscles, hair, and nails. Our muscles change, but we don't know when; Our hair and nails grow and we don't know when they grew, this is how the energy of Saturn works - gradually and slowly.

Saturn is an icy cold, windy and dry planet. This indicates that things become cold and dry when Saturn's influence begins. Once very warm relations, become cold; A hot business turns sluggish and things freeze like ice.

According to Hindu astrology, Saturn is said to be 'lame' which indicates the slow movement of the planet. Due to the influence of Saturn, various activities start slowing down and things do not move as fast as they were earlier. The downward movement of Saturn indicates that it brings the person down to earth and shows the real truth of life.

Due to the Saturnine effect airplanes, trains, and buses run late. The person will always reach late, the journey will be delayed, projects will not complete on time.

A strong Saturn indicates; honesty, reliability, truthfulness, balance in judgment, dutifulness, piousness, meditation, and concentration. Saturn bestows discipline, perseverance, responsibility, patience, endurance, stability, control, and frugality. Under the influence of Saturn, the person will grow a beard and do penance. It brings separation, silence, isolation, disease, old age, death, poverty, ugliness, and destruction.

Saturn is alert and careful; it rules over secret matters. It controls unfair judgment and brings balance. It brings limits and hates haste and works only after due consideration. Saturn is the protector and represents protection and security. A security guard must be tall and courageous. Persons under the influence of Saturn are tall and courageous.

Saturn is the son of the Sun but an enemy. Saturn is stubborn but does justice to everyone. Sun represents father and government. When there is a dispute between father and son or there is a problem with the government, then it is an indication of the relationship between Saturn and the Sun.

When a person is suffering from a period of despair or depression, then he goes into a dark room and reduces all hope, Saturn is darkness and despair. Therefore, to overcome such a situation, a person should not sit in a dark room with the lights off and he must remove all the negative energies around him. Saturn is isolation and filth; such persons will keep themselves in isolation and avoid cleaning their rooms and clothes. Saturn represents stale and cold foods; The person loses all interest in the food and starts eating stale food. Saturn is slow and lethargic; one loses all interest and becomes very slow in his daily activities. (Readers can refer to my book 'Psychology and Investment' to know more about depression)

People under the influence of Saturn prefer cold than hot. They prefer to eat ice cream than tea or coffee. They like to eat preserved foods, but remember Saturn is very stubborn. Excessive consumption of Saturnine products will make a person very stubborn. In my opinion, this could be one of the reasons why kids nowadays are so stubborn and they don't listen to their parents. Each planet controls certain food items and by eating such a thing, such a planet gets strength.

Saturn creates; obstacles, impediments, hindrances and will make the way difficult for the native. Human nature is that whatever you get for free, you will not appreciate it. Saturn teaches hard lessons to the person so that he gives importance to whatever he has gained or achieved.

Saturn represents fog, mist, and dust. People influenced by Saturn think a lot and cannot decide what to do. A weak Saturn indicates that the person is unable to take the right decision, their mind is clouded and they cannot see a clear picture. In case of any wrong deeds, a weak Saturnian person tries to spread dust on the matter and hide it, so that others also do not see a clear picture.

Saturn is exalted in Libra; Saturn represents balance and Libra is dance, the most desirable quality for dance is balance, it requires perfect balance. Everything on this earth is perfectly balanced and the dance of 'Nataraja' is going on continuously and the whole nature is presenting that dance that is perfectly balanced. Lord Saturn keeps balancing everything.

Libra is the marketplace and Saturn is honesty. The exaltation of Saturn indicates that the person will be honest in doing business.

Exalted Saturn indicates that one will give an equal share to all without any bias. Libra is a symbol of companionship, Librans are generous and help others, Saturn is respect, partnership will last long when you respect and help your partner. It indicates that the person will listen to the opinion of the public at large and will give importance to everyone's opinion and then will make a final decision, no one can influence the decision taken by Saturn. Aries represents single nature, while Libra represents partnership, these two zodiac signs are opposite to each other. Aries represents the singular soul and Saturn rules the masses. The element of Aries does not support the nature of Saturn and it becomes debilitated in this sign.

The position of Saturn in the horoscope indicates delay and struggle in matters related to the respective house, but Saturn always fulfils his promises. The transit of Saturn brings changes in the life of a person. Saturn has the power to destroy all material desires of a person and shows the true picture of life that only death is certain in this world, a very strong Saturn makes a person a hermit.

Affliction: If Saturn is afflicted the native will become lethargic, idle, lazy. It indicates denial, depression, disharmony, disappointment, dejection, despondency, a difference of opinion, etc. If it is heavily afflicted the native will become a cruel criminal. This creates distortion and paranoia. Saturn is dark, afflicted Saturn indicates underworld activities, sexual perversions, and unnatural sexual activities. The native will do any harm to others for the fulfillment of his desire. The native feels pleasure by causing pain to others and will use any kind of violence.

Body Parts and diseases: Hair and its growth, teeth, bladder, muscles, wrist, feet. Disease: Injury, operation, fracture, gallstone, anaemia, dryness, numbness, paralysis, muscular pain, toothache, joint pains, etc.

5.8 The Lunar Nodes - Rahu and Ketu

According to mythology, Lord Vishnu beheaded a demon named Swarnabhanu while he was sitting by the side of the gods at the time of distributing amrita (nectar). At that time, Swarnabhanu knew that the gods were not going to fulfill their promise of equitable distribution of nectar. He changed his entire outfit, began to look like a deity, and sat on the side where the deity was sitting to drink the nectar.

But Sun and Moon recognized him that he is not a deity, he is a demon and they informed Lord Vishnu. Immediately Lord Vishnu beheaded him but before that, he had drunk a few drops of nectar. That's why he became immortal. His head is called Rahu and his headless body becomes Ketu. The energy of these nodes is strange and mysterious and they always move in retrograde motion.

In Indian astrology Sun, Earth and Moon; three planets are involved to create the energy of Rahu and Ketu. The ecliptic is an imaginary line on the sky that marks the annual path of the Sun. The movement of the Earth and the Moon on their path produces enormous energy. The motion of the Moon when intersects this path, disturbs this energy. When the Moon's orbit crosses the ecliptic to the north, that point of intersection is called Rahu. Ketu is the point 180° apart from that intersection. Thus, Rahu and Ketu are the two imaginary points without any shape. This intersection creates the disturbance of two massive energies, any planet near these nodes gets disturbed and creates unusual events in the life of the native.

When a planet in transit crosses these nodes in the birth chart, there is a disturbance in the matter related to the respective house.

Some scriptures say that Rahu is exalted in Taurus and debilitated in Scorpio and Ketu is vice-versa. While some other classics say that Rahu is exalted in Gemini and debilitated in Sagittarius. Rahu is the co-ruler of Aquarius and its Mooltrikona sign is Virgo, while Ketu is the co-ruler of Scorpio and its Mooltrikona sign is Pisces. Both nodes represent tall in height and age of 100 years.

5.8.1 Rahu

Rahu - the north node of the Moon is a shadow planet. The direction of Rahu is South-West and stays 18 months in a sign. The caste of Rahu is Malechha (outcaste) and it represents all foreign elements like a foreign land, foreign caste, foreign people, etc. Rahu represents those reptiles having poison in their mouths like snakes, while Ketu represents those insects and creatures having poison in tails like scorpions. Rahu's gemstone is Gomedha.

The above mythology is very important to understand the characteristic of Rahu. Like Swarnabhanu had an intense desire to drink the nectar at any cost. Rahu signifies passion and obsession. To achieve this burning desire, he changed his face, his clothes, left the side of demons, joined the side of devatas, and took big risks with only one goal or better we can say with only one obsession – "I want this nectar at any cost" and he achieved it. But after achieving this, he lost his body shape.

The behavior of the person having a strong influence on Rahu is also the same. They are extremely obsessed to achieve their desire. For that purpose, they can cross any limit and don't care about the outcome and suffering. Just as Swarnabhanu lost the shape of his body in the end, similarly a person following the path of his obsession has to lose a lot from his life. One day he will get what he wants but for that, he will have to pay a very high price, like Swarnabhanu paid the price.

Mythology says that the Sun and the Moon recognized the demon sitting by the side of the gods and informed Lord Vishnu. After that, Sun and Moon became strong enemies of Rahu and Ketu, eclipse caused due to the transit of Rahu & Ketu and they have complete power to engulf Sun and Moon.

Sun and Moon represent our soul and mind. It means that if you run after your materialistic desire your soul and mind will become weak, your vision will become blurred and you will not be able to identify the truth. The smoke of materialism will gradually surround you and it will take over your soul and mind.

But if your soul and mind are strong then you can recognize the illusion created by Rahu. The person who has strong Sun and Moon in his horoscope can easily catch the hidden motive of the mischievous persons and keep himself away from all these. This is one of the many reasons; we worship the Sun and the Moon in Hindu culture so that our spirit and mind are strong and not eclipsed by material desire in the mundane world.

Rahu has only a mouth but no body. It indicates that a person with a strong influence of Rahu has a great desire but does not have the ability to digest it. Rahu always thinks about the future and its position in the horoscope indicates that the person wants to experience things that he does not have till now. Rahu means imbalance, mistakes; where a person learns from his experience. The Rahu-Ketu axis reflects the karmic relationship that we carry from our past lives – what we did and what we want to achieve. Rahu is such a power that does not listen to anyone's advice and is ready to cross any limit to fulfill his intense desire. Such natives do not care about the result, even if their head is cut off like Swarnabhanu.

Rahu is an airy and lawless planet. Rahu does not like any boundaries. A person having a strong influence of Rahu behaves the same. They don't want any control over themselves, they are ready to break any rule, and sometimes their behavior is over expansive. They don't like any questions and they don't want to give any explanations. They wander here and there like air and waste their time and energy.

Rahu indicates name, fame, overnight popularity, glamour, media sensation, material success, etc. All these represent illusion to the material world, and Rahu is the lord of all illusion. Due to the effect of Rahu, the person will show his face to the world and become popular. It controls the film and cinema industry, advertising industry, all modern computers, television, etc., and those jobs where a person is showing their face to the masses.

Rahu represents smoke, materialism, drugs, dark, and poison. Rahu is subtle, insensitive, deceptive, telling lies, harsh and voluptuous planet. Rahu indicates the person who will not think even twice of betraying his most trusted person. He can go to any extent to fulfill his desire.

Rahu represents paternal grandfather, quarrelsome person, greediness, cunningness, conspiracy, modern technology, foreigners, skin diseases, indigestion, restlessness, swelling in the body, problem-related with gas, black magic, phobias, gambling, speculation, leprosy, giddiness, fear from unknow, insanity, smuggling, underworld activities, terrorists, etc.

5.8.2 Ketu

Ketu - the south node, is the shadow planet of sudden and unexpected things. It also represents the experiences of our past lives, which we learned at a very high level and with mastery. It also represents a rigid and critical mindset where perfection is the highest goal at any cost. Ketu gemstone is Cat's eye also known as Lehsunia.

The symbol of Ketu is a flag that always stands vertically indicating the direction of the planet. A flag represents victory, but victory is not easy, victory on the battlefield is followed by great bloodshed and great sacrifices. The position of Ketu indicates that the native will get a victory after a lot of hard work and great sacrifice. Ketu provides clairvoyance and wisdom but after sufferings.

A strong Ketu blessed the native with powerful insights. It gives a power of intense concentration and deep penetration. This also represents vaccination where medicine is injected into the body. Ketu represents strong intuition, isolation, mediation, deep research, scientific jobs, drilling activities, etc. It belongs to those jobs where a person does with full concentration, to achieve their goal the person leaves the rest of the world and forgets everything. A strong Ketu is necessary to sit in the meditation for long hours. Ketu is a planet of seclusion and has no interest in the material world, the higher aspect of Ketu is salvation (Moksha).

Ketu represents inertia and strong attachment towards the past. It also represents a tendency where people want to live in their own world and do not want to change anything. Ketu represents Infra-Red Light, which is not visible to human eyes represents the mysterious functioning of this planet. It belongs to those diseases that are hidden and not easy to identify.

Ketu denotes separation, in which Ketu is placed it indicates separation from all materialistic things related to that house. Ketu is a planet of sudden events; a person has to face sudden changes in his life related to the matter of the concerned house. Ketu represents false sainthood, false knowledge, cheating, and humbugging profession, jealousy, hatred, deceit, murder, low-class sinful habits, etc. These nodes indicate all hidden criminal, anti-social activities that are done mostly at night.

5.9 The Eclipse

Eclipse is an important astronomical event and in astrology it is an important event that brings many changes and it deeply affects humans, society and country. It is important to consider in which Nakshatra the eclipse is taking place and if any natal planet is present in that Nakshatra, then a conjunction of less than five degrees is considered inauspicious.

The effect of a solar eclipse is more severe than a lunar eclipse, if there is any such conjunction in a horoscope, although not every eclipse is harmful to a person with this type of conjunction. It depends on which constellation the eclipse is taking place. Eclipses occur every year and the maximum number of solar and lunar eclipses in a year is seven. The question arises why eclipse is considered inauspicious?

The Sun represents the masculine energy of the universe and the Moon represents the feminine energy of the universe. It is only through the union of these two energies the process of creation continues in the world. Both of them are auspicious energies which protect the world from inauspiciousness. In the universe, not only good spirits are present but evil spirits are also present and they are looking for a chance to be born on earth, because nature prevents very lowly spirits from taking birth. During an eclipse, auspicious energy is absent from the environment for some time and these evil spirits get a chance to fulfill their desires.

Therefore, negative events, diseases, accidents and deaths increase around the eclipse. Hence, doing any auspicious work during eclipse is prohibited and giving birth to life is a very auspicious act which takes the human life forward. Therefore, sex is prohibited at the time of eclipse because auspicious energy is absent at that time and inauspicious energy can give birth to a crippled, impotent, criminal, murderer and an extremely cruel person.

5.10 Difference in Desire of Mars and Rahu

Mars is desire, and Rahu is also desire. Due to Martian energy, we move in this world and run behind our desire. So, what is the difference between these two desires?

Mars is a push. When a person runs behind his desire and utilizes his energy in a positive way, such desire is Martian. One works hard to fulfill such desire. But when a person does not want to work hard and wants to fulfill his desire by immoral means, that is Rahu.

Rahu is a criminal, Rahu is an illusion, Rahu is deceit, Rahu is an obsession, and Rahu does not want to listen to anyone's advice. Remember the story of Samudra Manthan (Churning the Ocean), Swarnabhanu wanted the nectar at any cost and he is not afraid of any punishment and cutting his head. He wanted to fulfill that desire by hook or by crook and he achieved that, but later he paid a very high price of separation of his head from his body. The chopped-off head of the Swarnabhanu is the final result of Rahu's obsession.

For example, if a student is working hard to clear an exam, he is utilizing Martian energy in a constructive manner. While another student is using deceitful methods to clear it, that is Rahu.

A person is working hard to get money, so he is improving his skills, such is Martian desire (a push to achieve something), while the other person decides to cheat people, indulge in fraudulent activities, indulge in theft and robbery, all such desires and activities are Rahu.

A person is looking for a promotion and to achieve such desire he starts working hard, he is improving his skills, he is learning new software, he is putting his Martian energy to achieve such an objective. On the other hand, there is another person who is using flattery to get a promotion rather than improving his skills. He starts using unethical means to fulfill his desire, that is Rahu.

Like Swarnabhanu had changed his face and even demi-gods were unable to recognize him, other than the Sun and the Moon. The person influenced with Rahu will change his face several times to fulfill his desire, and every face looks so real that it is very difficult to recognize such person's real face. Rahu has only one objective – "I want to fulfill this desire at any cost, and I am not afraid if my head is cut off for the fulfillment of such purpose." Remember, Rahu has no limit, he can cross any limit to fulfill his desire.

Rahu is temptation and false attraction. Rahu knows that my wish will not come true if I tell the truth. So, he always shows a rosy picture which attracts the temptation of the person. Rahu makes false promises, in fact, he does not care about promises, and he only cares about the achievement of his objective. The words spoken by Rahu have no meaning; he can turn at any time. But Mars is loyal, committed and never makes false promises.

Rahu always laughs how clever he is in deceiving others, how he fools others on false promises. But if Mars is unable to fulfill a promise, he regrets it and immediately says sorry to that person.

Rahu wants to enjoy on the wealth and misery of others, and will fight how not to give. But Mars, the sibling of Earth will never enjoy the wealth of others, and just as Earth has the quality of giving, Mars has the same quality. He returns the others possessions with full honesty.

Mars is the protector, who uses his force and weapon always for protection. But Rahu always uses his power only for the fulfillment of his desire. Mars is ready to sacrifice himself for others, Rahu is also not afraid of death but, only to fulfill his desire and never do any sacrifice.

Rahu is not afraid of dying and being killed, but his purpose must be served. But Mars, the protector will leave the path if he finds that the purpose is wrong.

Mars always thinks about others to protect and is ready to give. Rahu never thinks about others and is always ready to snatch from others.

When a person uses Martian energy to fulfill his desire, which is a constructive path, he feels rejoices and shows his achievement to others. When a person uses Rahu's energy to fulfill his desire, immediately after getting the desired object he disappears because Rahu does not have any existence. Others come to know his true face only when his desires are fulfilled.

5.11 Shanivat Rahu & Kujavat Ketu

Phaladeepika says, "Shanivat Rahu and Kujavat Ketu" i.e. in giving effect Rahu is similar to Saturn and Ketu is similar to Mars (Chapter 8, Shloka 34). The above statement has a very important meaning in Vedic astrology, which has been written by our ancient sages after understanding the planetary behaviour and human mind very deeply.

5.11.1 Shanivat Rahu

The sutra states that Rahu behaves like Saturn or Rahu gives the results of Saturn. When one person behaves like another person it means that there are similarities or some common qualities between them and they like to support each other to achieve their objective. The same thing applies to the planets, but when seen on the surface, the behaviour of Saturn and Rahu appears opposite to each other.

Saturn and Rahu: The Opposite Qualities

Following are some of the opposite qualities of both the planets;

1. Rahu is greedy and selfish and Saturn represents contentment.

2. Rahu is hungry for materialistic things and Saturn is indifferent.

3. Rahu forces the person to run after material desires and Saturn forces the person to give up every material desire.

4. Rahu indicates obsession and Saturn indicates apathy.

5. Rahu is fast and Saturn is slow.

6. Rahu represents liquor and drugs and Saturn represents diseases and death.

7. Rahu snatches things from others and Saturn isolates from everything and brings renunciation.

There seems to be no connection between these two energies. But when we look deeply, we will find that both of them are connected.

Saturn and Rahu: The Similarities

Rahu represents excessive and unfulfilled desires and the person runs around the world to fulfill these desires, in this process, Saturn is following Rahu. For example; Rahu represents alcohol and drugs and when a person takes alcohol and drugs he is inviting diseases. Hence, wherever Rahu goes, Saturn stands behind him. You consume alcohol and drugs and Saturn will soon give you diseases and death. The ancient sutra rightly says that Rahu gives the results of Saturn.

Rahu forces the person to go on the path of greed and later Saturn puts him in legal trouble and imprisonment. When Saturn wants to send a person to jail, he orders Rahu to tempt the person and then Rahu creates a rosy picture of a beautiful dreamy world and the person gets trapped. People lose their money and become poor because of greed. Rahu brings temptation and Saturn brings poverty, they both are connected.

The futility of material desire is realized only when one's hands get burnt, the race for attainment continues till the hands get burnt. Renunciation is possible only after the experience of burning of chasing desires, Rahu paves the way for Saturn.

When a person's wealth increases, his ego starts increasing and Saturn destroys every ego. So, Saturn sends Rahu to portray a rosy picture of some lucrative investments, due to greed such people get easily tempted and lose their money, and later become down-to-earth people. Yes, Rahu acts as an agent of Saturn.

Rahu is fast and Saturn is slow and brings obstacles. Rahu can cross any limit and when the limits are crossed then accidents become possible. Faster speeds mean that accidents are more likely to occur, so barriers are necessary to slow down speeds. Everything is good if it is within limits. Hence, Saturn always stands behind Rahu. Saturn creates hindrances and will make the way difficult for the natives. Human nature is that whatever you get for free, you will not appreciate it. Saturn teaches tough lessons to the person so that he gives importance to whatever he has gained or achieved.

Rahu is an extrovert and Saturn is an introvert. No person can become an introvert without experiencing the futility of worldly desires. Every experience makes us a mature and introverted person and what we do not have we run for it and as soon as it comes in hand it immediately becomes worthless. Hence, Rahu and Saturn move together, and entry of Rahu i.e. entry of Saturn is inevitable. Saturn teaches us to control things and bring limits.

Rahu snatches things from others and people start hating the one who snatches them. People try to avoid snatchers, love for the giver and hatred for the taker begins to arise automatically. The snatcher creates isolation and Saturn separates that person from others. That's why thieves and robbers get separated from the society. Rahu is unbalanced energy and Saturn removes all that prevents balance. Therefore, Saturn removes these thieves and robbers from the society and bring balance.

Saturn is exalted in Libra; Saturn represents balance and Libra represents dance, the most desirable quality for dance is balance, it requires perfect balance. Rahu creates imbalance and Saturn always maintains balance. Everything on earth is perfectly balanced and the dance of 'Nataraja' is going on continuously and the whole nature is presenting that dance that is perfectly balanced. Lord Saturn keeps balancing everything and his agents help him to achieve this.

5.11.2 Kujavat Ketu

Kujavat Ketu means Ketu is similar to Mars or Ketu gives the results of Mars. Ketu is the planet of separation and Mars represents action, energy, and fighting.

Mars – The Supreme Commander

Mars is considered as commander-in-chief in the planetary cabinet. The job of a commander is to follow the orders given by the king where action is always important. Therefore, Mars never think twice and does not care about the sufferings and consequences, fulfilment of the order or achieving the target is always important and it has to be done at any cost.

The focus of Mars is always on achievement and this energy shows achievements to the world, but the greatest achievement is salvation which is the ultimate achievement and is represented by Ketu. Ketu needs the energy of Mars to achieve its goal. Therefore, the sutra says that Ketu behaves like Mars or results in the energy of Mars, it means that higher energy is required on the spiritual path.

When there is a task it has to be done, when there is an obstacle it has to be removed. To achieve a difficult task or remove an obstacle requires energy. Mars does not bother about how the task has been achieved or how the obstacle has been removed. Mars only considers how to achieve the target.

Mars creates top business executives who are focused on how to achieve goals and do not hesitate to fire non-performers. Separation is the characteristic of Ketu that indicates the final outcome and the result of Ketu requires the energy of Mars. Therefore, corporate bosses tell their employees to either show their achievements or get away from the company. Ketu gives the result of Mars, either separation or taking the flag, and showing achievement to everyone because the symbol of Ketu is the flag.

Ketu – The Headless Planet

Ketu is a headless planet, and the head works to think and control. Our head controls every organ of the body and when the head is gone it means such a person has no control over his body. In spirituality, no head means no ego and the path of salvation requires surrender of ego to God. Therefore, Ketu is known as the planet of salvation.

Ketu is related to the deeds of previous birth. It shows inertia and attachment to the past. It indicates resistance towards changes and the people are ready to fight if someone intervenes and wants to bring about some changes. The planet of separation is not separated in characteristics from Mars.

Few More Examples

The energy of Ketu is highly influenced by the energy of Mars, which means whatever house Ketu is in, the person does not think about the consequences and acts without pondering. When Ketu wants to separate something, it behaves like Mars. We can understand the meaning of Kujavat Ketu with the help of some more examples;

Suppose, two are close friends and Ketu wants to separate them, then a fight starts between them on any issue, and most of the time issue is related to the past because Ketu represents past. Here, Ketu is behaving like Mars, they both fight without thinking about the consequences and separate from each other.

For example; If Ketu is in the 11th house then the person gets separated from his friend after a fight related to some past issue. When Ketu is situated in the tenth house it means that such a person will leave his workplace, but before that, discord starts in the office and that atmosphere forces the person to leave the workplace. Ketu in the first house indicates that the person accumulates all the incidents for which he wants to take revenge, but the energy of Ketu does not come to the surface easily, so it gets accumulated. One day the person becomes explosive by remembering all the incidents that happened in the past, because Ketu represents explosion.

When husband and wife separate from each other, even before that a heated argument starts between the two related to the past incidents. Both of them fight without thinking about the consequences and their every fight invites Ketu which behave like Mars at this time and ultimately brings separation. Ketu also indicates silence and silence spreads after separation. We should analyze Ketu with the possibility that the character of Mars is also hidden there. Hence, the ancient sutra rightly says that Ketu is similar to Mars in giving effect.

There is no separation without fighting and this is true whether it is between friends, husband-wife, family matter, or state matter. If separation is not to happen then fighting will have to stop. If the energy of Ketu has to be pacified then Mars will have to be pacified first.

Ketu and Mars – Few Other Characteristics

Ketu represents intuition and Mars is a bachelor planet and represents celibacy. The sutra indicates that the power of intuition develops only when a person follows the path of celibacy. Ketu represents salvation, the word Kujavat Ketu indicates salvation is possible and will happen only on the path of celibacy.

Ketu is a planet of separation and if it is placed in the 7th house, it not only indicates separation from partner (other factors have to be seen) but also forces the person to follow the path of celibacy. It indicates late marriage, self-restraint, or monkhood. It also indicates the religious nature of the person and such a person follows the religious rules with full devotion.

A strong Ketu blessed the native with powerful insights. It gives a power of intense concentration and deep penetration. Ketu represents mediation, deep research, scientific jobs, drilling activities, etc. and Mars indicates energy. A high level of energy is required to do these kinds of jobs; therefore, these people automatically get separated from the rest of the world. The other characteristics of Ketu also become visible in their personality, like; intuition, silence, late-night activity, etc.

The warrior planet Mars represents courage, passion, strength, and aggression. It represents arms and weapons that are used by army and police personnel. These people wear uniforms that create separation from others. Ketu indicates separation, when a person wears a uniform he automatically gets separated from others. Ketu is a planet of sudden events, due to weapon death happen suddenly. These examples indicate how the energy of Ketu works and it is highly associated with the energy of Mars.

The symbol of Ketu is flag and armed soldiers carry flag with them which is a symbol of victory. Every victory requires courage, strength, and sacrifice. Ketu is the goal that can be achieved by following the path of Mars. Ketu represents the end result and Mars represents the path, whether one's goal is in the material world or the spiritual, but victory can be achieved only by the proper utilization of the Martian energy.

On the Downside

A malefic Ketu represents false sainthood, false knowledge, cheating, humbugging profession, deceit, murder, and low-class sinful activities, etc. These nodes (Rahu & Ketu) indicate all criminal, anti-social activities that are done mostly at night. The people who are engaged in these activities carry weapons and they keep it at hidden places. When the energy is high and the brain is absent then the person becomes merciless. They become tyrant and mass murderers who use weapons to make many people headless.

Chapter 6

Key Features of Planets

6.1 Planetary Relationship

Planets	Friends	Neutral	Enemies
Sun	Moon, Mars, Jupiter	Mercury	Venus, Saturn, Rahu
Moon	Sun, Mercury	Mars, Jupiter, Venus, Saturn	Rahu, Ketu
Mars	Sun, Moon, Jupiter	Venus, Saturn	Mercury, Rahu
Mercury	Sun, Venus, Rahu	Mars, Jupiter, Saturn	Moon
Jupiter	Sun, Moon, Mars	Saturn, Rahu	Mercury, Venus
Venus	Mercury, Saturn, Rahu	Mars, Jupiter	Sun, Moon
Saturn	Mercury, Venus, Rahu	Jupiter	Sun, Moon, Mars
Rahu	Venus, Mercury, Saturn	Jupiter	Sun, Moon, Mars
Ketu	Venus, Mercury, Saturn	Jupiter	Sun, Moon, Mars

6.2 Temporary Relationship

Temporary Friends: Planets that happen to be located on the 2nd, 3rd, 4th, 12th, 11th, and 10th from one another become temporary friends.

Temporary Enemies: Planets located in houses 1st, 7th, 5th, 9th, 6th, and 8th from any planet become its temporal enemies.

Both types of relationships are considered while examining a horoscope and a combined relationship is obtained which is as under;

- Friend + Friend = Great Friend

- Friend + Neutral = Friend

- Friend + Enemy = Neutral

- Enemy + Neutral = Enemy

- Enemy + Enemy = Great Enemy

6.3 Natural Karak

House	Natural Karak
1st	Sun
2nd	Jupiter
3rd	Mars
4th	Moon
5th	Jupiter
6th	Mars
7th	Venus
8th	Saturn
9th	Jupiter
10th	Sun, Mercury, Jupiter, Saturn
11th	Jupiter
12th	Saturn

6.4 Karakas in Jaimini Astrology

According to Jaimini astrology, the karaka is of great importance and it varies for each horoscope. The determination of the karaka is based on the longitude of the planet from the beginning of the respective sign. Following are the seven main karakas –

i) Atmakaraka – This is the planet having the highest longitude in a sign. The strength of this planet reflects the general strength of the horoscope. The natural Atmakaraka is considered the Sun. For example; suppose among all planets the Moon has the highest longitude is 27 degrees in Aries. So, Moon is considered as an Atmakaraka in this horoscope.

ii) Amatya karaka - The planet in a sign having the second-highest longitude becomes the Amatya karaka. There is no natural Amatyakaraka but Mercury is considered for the same.

iii) Bhratru karaka - The planet in a sign having the third-highest longitude becomes the Bhratru karaka. It rules over the events pertaining to our siblings. Mars is considered a natural Bhratru karaka.

iv) Matru karaka - The fourth planet in order of longitude becomes Matru karaka. Moon (is considered as Mother) is the natural Matru karaka.

v) Putra karaka – The fifth planet in order of longitude becomes Putra karaka. It is considered the lord of children and Jupiter is the natural significator for this karaka.

vi) Gnati karaka – The next planet in order of degree becomes Gnati karaka. It is considered the lord of relations and Mars is considered as natural significator of this karaka.

vii) Dara karaka - The planet least in order of degree becomes Dara karaka, an indicator of spouse, marriage, and partnership. Venus is the natural significator of Dara karaka.

While determining the karaka do not multiply with the longitude of the sign, consider only the position of the planet in a sign up to a degree, minutes and seconds.

6.5 Planets in Groups

a) Natural Malefic and Benefic

Sun, Mars, Saturn, and the Moon (within less than 72° distance from Sun) are treated as natural malefic. Moon other than of the nature referred to above, Mercury, Jupiter, and Venus are natural benefics. In the case of Mercury, however, if it is in association with malefic it is treated as a malefic, if with benefics then treated as benefic.

b) Maturity Age of Planets

Planets	Maturity Age
Sun	22
Moon	24
Mars	28
Mercury	32
Jupiter	16
Venus	25
Saturn	36
Rahu	42
Ketu	49

c) Vegetables and Fruits

Planets	Vegetable and Fruits
Sun	Chillies, Reddish etc.
Moon	All Cold substances and tender fruits and vegetables
Mars	All substances of fleshy nature and groundnut, Grains etc.
Mercury	Plantains, Brinjals, Ladies Finger, Beetroot etc.
Jupiter	All native roots and bulbs, pumpkin, plantains etc.
Venus	All exotic vegetables, potatoes, cabbages etc.
Saturn	Bittergourd, Onions, Drumstick, Betel leaves, Tobacco etc.
Rahu	Snakegourd, Flavoury substances, Garlic etc.
Ketu	-

d) Tastes

Planet	Tastes
Sun	Pungent taste (e.g. onion, ginger, pepper)
Moon	Saline taste (e.g. sea salt, rock salt)
Mars	Bitter taste (e.g. karela, neem leaves)
Mercury	Mixed taste
Jupiter	Sweetness (e.g. sugar, sweets, dates)
Venus	Sour taste (e.g. lemon, oranges, tamarind)
Saturn	Astringent taste (e.g. plantain, pomegranate)

6.6 Planetary Strengths and Weaknesses

a) Strength of Planets based on its degrees

A planet in the first or last two degrees of a sign is said to be powerless for material gains and will not give good material results to that planet or the houses ruled by it.

Various states of Planets as per its degrees -

Planetary States	Degree
Young Planet	: Between 10° to 22°
Adolescence Planet	: Between 2° to 10°
Old Planet	: Between 22° to 28°
Dead Planet	: Between 28° to 30° and 0° to 2°

b) Maran Karak Sthana

Some places in the horoscope are not suitable for planets because that place is against the tendency of that planet and they feel uncomfortable just by sitting there. We also do not like to sit in some places and many times we refuse to sit there, but what happens when we have to sit there forcefully, our whole mind gets disturbed. Similarly, the planets located at the Maran Karak place also do not work properly and create disturbance in the life of the native.

•Sun:12th house is the Maran Karak Sthan

• Moon: 8th house is the Maran Karak Sthan

• Mars: 7th house is the Maran Karak Sthan

• Mercury: 7th house is the Maran Karak Sthan

• Jupiter: 3rd house is the Marana Karaka Sthana

• Venus: 6th house is the Maran Karak Sthan

• Saturn: 1st house is the Maran Karak Sthan

• Rahu: 9th house is the Marana Karaka Sthana

c) Yog Karak

The Planet becomes Yoga Karak when it owns both Kendra and Trikona from any ascendant without owning the Dusthana houses (6th, 8th, and 12th). Kendra means 1st, 4th, 7th and 10th houses from Ascendant and Trikona means 1st,5th, and 9th houses from the Ascendant. In Zodiac, the following Yoga Karak planets for different ascendants are as follows:

• Taurus: Saturn - 9th and 10th lord

• Cancer: Mars - 5th and 10th lord

- Leo: Mars - 4th and 9th lord

- Libra: Saturn - 4th and 5th lord

- Capricorn: Venus - 5th and 10th lord

- Aquarius: Venus - 4th and 9th lord

d) Vargottam Planet

When a planet is in the same sign in the birth chart and the Navamsa chart, then that planet is called Vargottam planet. It is made up of two words 'Varga' and 'Uttam'. Vargottam means that the planet has become very powerful in the horoscope of the person. Whenever a planet is Vargottam, the qualities of that planet become a part of the person's characteristics. Locating a planet in the same sign as D1 and D9 is the primary role in finding Vargottam planet. A badly placed planet in Vargottam means it can give more bad results.

e) Exchange of Signs

When two planets occupy each other's signs, they are said to be in exchange. This is a very powerful condition and will greatly enhance the houses the planets occupy as well as the houses the planets rule. Not only can the planets be said to act as if placed in their own sign, but the affairs of two houses in exchange work together.

6.7 Planetary Aspects

According to Hindu astrology, a planet cannot aspect any other planet or bhava with 30° in front of it and 60° behind it. The aspect starts at 30° in front of a planet and it stops at 300° from the planet.

All Planets aspect 7th house from the position occupied by them. However, Mars, Jupiter, Saturn, and Rahu have special aspects besides the 7th aspect. The planetary aspects are as under:

- Sun, Mercury, Venus - 7th

- Mars - 4th, 7th, 8th,

- Jupiter and Rahu- 5th, 7th, 9th

- Saturn - 3rd, 7th, 10th

6.8 Aspect of Signs

All movable signs aspect all fixed signs, except the adjacent ones. All fixed signs aspect all movable signs except the adjacent ones. Common signs aspect each other. For example, Aries aspects the fixed sign Leo, Scorpio, and Aquarius but not Taurus being an adjacent sign. Taurus aspects Cancer, Libra, and Capricorn but not Aries, an adjacent sign.

Aspecting Sign	Aspected Sign
Aries	: Leo, Scorpio and Aquarius
Taurus	: Cancer, Libra and Capricorn
Gemini	: Virgo, Sagittarius and Pisces
Cancer	: Scorpio, Aquarius and Taurus
Leo	: Libra, Capricorn and Aries
Virgo	: Sagittarius, Pisces and Gemini
Libra	: Aquarius, Taurus and Leo
Scorpio	: Capricorn, Aries and Cancer
Sagittarius	: Pisces, Gemini and Virgo
Capricorn	: Taurus, Leo and Scorpio
Aquarius	: Aries, Cancer and Libra
Pisces	: Gemini, Virgo and Sagittarius

6.9 Retrograde Planet

The condition of a planet when it appears to move backward is called Retrograde or Vakri (in Sanskrit). The word retrograde comes from the Latin word "Retogradus", which means "Going backward". The Sun and the Moon never retrograde while Rahu and Ketu always move in retrograde motion. Hence, the rest of the five planets Mercury, Venus, Mars, Jupiter, and Saturn are considered here.

Retrograde motion is not real but an apparent change in the moment of the planet. Normally, the planets always move around the Sun in the same direction and west-to-east through the stars at night. But at a time, the motion changes and they move east-to-west through the stars. This motion occurs when a faster-moving planet catches up to and passes a slower-moving planet. The retrograde motion continues for a short time and then the motion switches back to direct motion.

Hindu astrology says that a planet either benefic or malefic becomes stronger and more powerful when they become retrograde. If a planet is exalted and retrogrades it gives the result of a debilitated planet and vice versa. Retrograde or backward step means time to review and reassessments the areas of life in which house the planet is retrograde and completes your pending assignments.

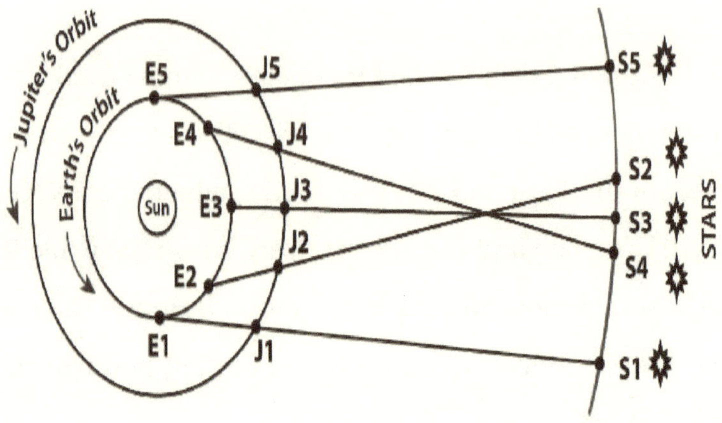

Let us understand the whole concept with an example. Suppose, you decided to travel from Mumbai to Delhi with a few other friends in different cars to complete a certain task there. After travelling for about a few kilometres, you suddenly remember that you have left the water tap open in your house, the electric lights are on, and have forgotten to lock the door. Now you cannot go any further, you will have to take a U-turn and return to your home. Your return speed will be higher than your earlier one. Your task is to finish all the uncompleted assignments quickly, but your friends are moving towards their goal and they have gone far ahead of you. But what about those tasks that you decided to complete before the start of this journey. Now your speed is again fast to complete the rest of the assignments. This is the work of the retrograde planet in the horoscope. When you first went out with your friends, your mind was calm but now your mind cannot remain calm during this whole process. Retrograde planet means lack of peace.

When Mahadasha and Antardasha of a retrograde planet start, the life of the person does not remain normal, the earlier pace of life is disturbed and various changes start coming. Many of us must have noticed that the memory of some unfinished work comes shortly after starting a new journey. You have not gone very far and suddenly your mind remembers the unfinished task. We just started the journey and we have to come back to complete the pending tasks that we have left in our previous lives. Therefore, the retrograde planet is very powerful.

The universe is a great recorder. It records everything, all the sounds we have produced so far, good or bad, it has recorded, and we cannot proceed further with the heavy burden of unfinished assignments. The retrograde planet forces us to complete our work and then move on.

Planet	No. of Retrograde Days	No. of Stationery Days
Saturn	140	5
Jupiter	120	5
Mars	80	3-4
Venus	42	2
Mercury	24	1

6.10 Combust Planet

When a planet gets close in conjunction with the Sun, then the said state is called combustion. Due to the heat of the Sun, the energy of the planet gets burnt and it is unable to function independently. This type of combustion destroys the basic importance of the planet and it becomes powerless. But the Sun's energy only burns the materialistic thing of the planet, the planet's characteristics still exist and it merges with the Sun. The Sun has the independent right to make decisions in the house in which the planet is combust. The Sun has become more subtle and powerful which influences the native to work on the mind than physical activity. Suppose, in the case of mercury combustion, the Sun's decisions are influenced by Mercurian traits.

The planet which will be together at equal degrees near the Sun, that planet will be considered to be completely combust. The planet which is at a distance of 8 degrees from the Sun will be considered as half-combust and the planet which is at a distance of 15 degrees from the Sun will be considered as fully rising.

6.11 Planets and Transit Time

a) Average Daily Motion of Planets

Moon	: 13 degrees 11 minute	Mars	:	33 Min 28 Sec
Mercury	: 1 Min 23 Sec	Jupiter	:	4 Min 59 Sec
Venus	: 1 Min 12 Sec	Saturn	:	2 Min 0 sec
Sun	: 59 Min 8 Sec	Rahu-Ketu	:	3 Min 11 Sec

b) Time taken by planets to complete one revolution & to change a sign

	To Complete one revolution		To change a sign
Planet	Days	Years	(Approx.)
Mercury	88	0.2	15 Days
Venus	224.7	0.6	28 Days
Earth (Sun)	365.25	1	30 Days
Mars	687	1.9	45 Days
Jupiter	4332.8	11.9	1 Year
Saturn	10755.7	29.5	2.5 Years

6.12 Effect of Planets before their Sign Change

Sun	: Starts giving results 5 days before
Moon	: Starts giving results of 1.25 hours before
Mars	: Starts giving results 8 days before
Mercury	: Starts giving results 7 days before
Venus	: Starts giving results 7 days before
Jupiter	: Starts giving results 2 months before
Saturn	: Starts giving results 6 months before
Rahu & Ketu	: Starts giving results 3 months before

Also,

• It is assumed that Sun and Mars give results with full power in 1st drekkana (0° to 10°) of sign.

• Jupiter and Venus give results with full strength in 2nd drekkana (10° to 20°) of sign.

6.13 Shadbala

Planets produce their results on the basis of their strength or weakness in the horoscope. Shadbala is a mathematical model for measuring the power received from 6 different sources.

1. Sthana Bala (Positional Strength)

2. Dig Bala (Directional Strength)

3. Kala Bala (Time Strength)

4. Chesta Bala (Motion Strength)

5. Naisargika Bala (Natural Strength)

6. Drig Bala (Aspectual Strength)

1. Sthana Bala (Positional Strength): Sthana means "position" or "standing", the power of the planet increases only because of its position and the planet which has the highest points in the Sthana Bala is very evident in the character of the person.

The Components of Sthana Bala (Positional Strength):

i) Uchcha Bala: The strength of Ucca Bala measures how close the planet is to its degree of exaltation.

ii) Saptavarga Bala: The power of Saptavarga Bala is measured according to the dignity of the planet in the seven divisional charts.

iii) Sama/Visama Bala: The strength of the planets in the birth chart and navamsa chart assesses whether the female planets are in the female sign and the male planets are in the male sign.

iv) Kendradi Bala: The strength of Kendradi Bala is based on the position of planets in angular (1,4,7,10), succedent (2,5,8,11), cadent (3,6,9,12) houses.

v) Dreskana Bala: The strength of this Bala is assessed on the basis of the position of male, female and eunuch planets in dreshkana.

2. Dig Bala (Directional Strength): Planets get strengths or weaknesses only by positing in some specific direction. The Sun and Mars get directional strength in the 10th house and weakness in the 4th house. 10th house is also known as Midheaven. At noon, the Sun reaches there and it is extremely powerful during that time. Mars, the commander-in-chief gets directional strength here and it represents that the native is full of energy and leadership quality.

Moon and Venus get directional strength in the 4th house and weakness in the 10th house. The 4th house is the house of mother, peace, happiness, and comfort. Moon represents mother and peace and Venus provides comfort. The 4th house is also called the nadir point in the horoscope and it is the time of midnight. During this time the Moon gets full strength and Moon in the 4th house indicates a high level of feminine quality of the native. Venus in 4th bestow the person with all luxuries at home.

Jupiter and Mercury get directional strength in the 1st house, which is the house of self. It represents the individuality of the person with independent thinking, communication, learning, and wisdom.

Saturn gets directional strength in the 7th house, which is the house of partner. Saturn in 7th indicates delay in marriage or age difference with the partner. The placement of Saturn indicates hard work and maintenance of discipline in life.

3. Kala Bala (Time Strength): Planets gain their strength based on the time when the native has taken birth. Some planets are stronger when born during the day and some are stronger at night. When Dasha of those planets that are strong in Kala Bala are running that creates significant changes in the person's life. The Sun, Jupiter, and Venus are strong during the daytime, and Mars, Moon, and Saturn are strong during nighttime. Mercury is strong at the time of sunrise and sunset. Benefics are strong during the bright half and malefics are strong during the dark half of the lunar month.

4. Chesta Bala (Motion Strength): The movement of the planets is considered under Chesta Bala. The slow-moving planet gets a high Chesta Bala value while the fast-moving planet gets a low Chesta Bala value. The Sun and the Moon do not get Chesta Bala values. They always move in direct motion and do not retrograde.

5. Naisargika Bala (Natural Strength): The natural strength of the planets is considered under this Bala. Each planet has its own natural strengths and weaknesses and a planet with high natural strength is considered strong.

6. Drig Bala (Aspectual Strength): The aspectual strength is considered under this Bala. When a planet is Aspected by natural benefics Jupiter and Venus, it becomes powerful while the aspect of malefics weakens them.

Chapter 7

Important Yogas

7.1 Amala Yoga

This yoga is caused by the presence of a natural benefic in the tenth house from the Lagna or the Moon. The person is helpful, charitable, enjoy pleasures, fame, reputation, and will lead a prosperous life.

7.2 Budha – Aditya Yoga

When Mercury combines with the Sun, such a combination is called Budha-Aditya Yoga. The person is skillful, highly intelligent, achieves respect and reputation in his life, and is surrounded by all comforts and happiness.

7.3 Gaja-Kesari Yoga

A Gaja-Kesari yoga is produced when Jupiter occupies a Kendra position (1,4,7,10) in relation to the Moon or the Lagna and avoids debilitation, combustion, and inimical sign. One born in Gaj-

Kesari Yoga will be illustrious, virtuous, wealthy, splendorous, intelligent, scholarly, and enjoys long-lasting fame.

7.4 Guru Mangal Yoga

When Jupiter and Mars are in conjunction or mutually aspect, then Guru-Mangal Yoga is formed. Jupiter is the direction and Mars is the energy. When energy gets direction, it gives fruitful results. Mars is action and Jupiter is wisdom; this yoga brings the quality for accurate judgment of risk and takes action accordingly. Mars is aggression, Jupiter in knowledge; this yoga presents sharp intelligence with the ability to observe the situation in depth. This yoga is powerful for conquering enemies, creating wealth, and living life purposefully. The house on which the combined aspect of these two planets falls shows the combined effect of both the planets.

7.5 Shubh Kartari and Pap Kartari

Shubh Kartari Yoga is formed when a planet or a house is surrounded by benefic planets from both its sides and Paap Kartari Yog is formed when a planet or a house is surrounded by malefic planets on both sides without any beneficial aspect. This yoga can be understood better with a situation when both of the neighbours are good then they will help and when both of the neighbours are bad then no help will come, they will affect the house and create unnecessary problems. Shubh kartari yoga increases the auspiciousness of the planet or house while pap kartari yoga tends to cause difficulty for that planet or house.

7.6 The Chandra Yoga

The Yogas arising from the Moon are as follows:

7.6.1 Sunapha Yoga

When the second house from the Moon is occupied by any planet, other than the Sun, the Sunapha yoga arises. This yoga bestows upon the native status, wealth, and capacity to earn his fortune.

7.6.2 Anapha Yoga

When the 12th house from the Moon is occupied by any planet, other than the Sun, Anapha yoga is created. The person has good character, devoid of disease, good name, enjoy life and comfort.

7.6.3 Durdhara Yoga

When both 2nd and 12thhouse from the Moon are occupied by any planet, other than the Sun, this yoga is formed. This yoga confers upon the native wealth, vehicles, comforts, and freedom from enemies.

7.6.4 Kemdrum Yoga

When no planet conjuncts the Moon, none of these two houses from the Moon are occupied by any planet and no planet is in Kendra from the Moon. The presence of the Sun in these two houses does not make any difference, yoga tends to give a very unhappy life. The native is poor, mean, wicked, and suffers from physical illness.

7.6.5 Chandradhi Yoga

This yoga is formed when all the three houses 6th, 7th, and 8th from the Moon are occupied by natural benefics (Mercury, Jupiter, and Venus). This yoga gives rise to high status, the command of an army, kingship, and governmental recognition. This yoga further ensures good health, long life, and prosperity.

7.6.6 Dhana Yoga from the Moon

In case an entire lot of the natural benefic planets are located in the upachaya house (3,6,10,11) from both the ascendant and the Moon the man is extremely rich. If two of the benefics are located he is highly rich. If only one is in these houses he is moderately rich. This yoga has powerful powers as it makes a person rich even if he is born in Kemdrum Yoga etc.

7.7 The Ravi Yoga

7.7.1 Veshi Yoga

This yoga arises when any planet, other than the Moon, occupies the second house from the Sun. When benefics constitute this yoga, the native is eloquent, wealthy and an annihilator of opponents. When malefic do so, the native is destitute and associated with wicked people.

7.7.2 Voshi Yoga

This yoga arises when any planet, other than the Moon, occupies the 12th house as reckoned from the Sun. When this yoga is caused by benefics, the native is intelligent, learned, strong, wealthy, and engaged in scientific pursuits. Malefics causing this yoga led to cruel nature, ugly looks, and poor intelligence.

7.7.3 Ubhayachari Yoga

This yoga is caused when planets other than the Moon occupy the second and the 12th houses from the Sun. When this yoga is caused by benefics, the native is capable of shouldering great responsibilities, great learning, balanced outlook, wealthy, good looking, and blessed with numerous objects of pleasure. When this yoga is caused by malefics, the native is sickly, servile, destitute, and of a wicked disposition.

7.8 Pancha-Mahapurush Yoga

Pancha Mahapurush Yoga are caused when Mars, Mercury, Jupiter, Venus, and Saturn possess the greatest strength and occupy their exaltation sign, moolktrikona sign or own sign in a Kendra houses 1,4,7 and 10.

7.8.1 Ruchak Yoga

Ruchak yoga forms when Mars, exalted or in its own house, is located in a Kendra from the Lagna. Mars signifies courage, confidence, younger brothers, land, army, and ambition. When this yoga exists in a chart, this person has a lot of positive effects of Mars. The native has an attractive body and is a health-conscious person.

7.8.2 Bhadra Yoga

Bhadra yoga forms when Mercury is in either Gemini or Virgo as its own sign or exaltation sign. Mercury is the planet of communication and analysis. It is also the planet of intellect and studies. A highly positive influence of Mercury is seen in a chart when this yoga is present. The person will be good in intelligence, education, and eloquence in communication.

7.8.3 Hamsa Yoga

Hamsa yoga is formed when Jupiter is in Kendra in its own house, exalted house, or in mooltrikona house. Jupiter represents religion, happiness, wealth, spirituality, and higher studies. When

Jupiter creates this yoga, the person has a lot of fortune, easy gains, and follows the path of spirituality.

7.8.4 Malavya Yoga

Malavya yoga is formed when Venus occupies its own sign or its exalted sign in Kendra. Venus indicates, beauty, love, money, fine arts, and luxury. This is the best yoga for marital pleasure, happiness, and prosperous life. A person with Malavya Yoga is inclined towards all the activities of the planet Venus and fulfills his material desires. He is a broad-minded and selfless person desirous of spiritual advancement.

7.8.5 Shasha Yoga

Shasha Yoga is formed when Saturn is in Kendra i.e., in its zodiac Capricorn, Mooltrikon Aquarius, or exalted Libra. Saturn is a planet of discipline, fear, it is cruel, stubborn, and brave. This yoga brings the person in authority and power, the person will have a tendency to rule over others and shows no mercy. This yoga makes the person an industrialist, a war contractor, an underworld don, a great leader, a ruthless dictator, etc.

7.9 Raj Yoga

Raj yoga forms when the lords of the Kendra are related to the lords of the triangle by; Mutual aspects, conjunctions, exchange of houses, and the presence of one planet in the other's house. It is said that the Kendra (houses 1,4,7,10) belong to Lord Vishnu while the triangles (houses 1,5,9) belong to Goddess Lakshmi. Raja Yoga is formed by the union of two lords (center and triangle). The lagna is considered as both the center and the triangle. Some other Raja yoga –

- When Mars, Sun, Saturn, Jupiter are in exaltation and one of them is in the ascendant

- When three or more planets should be in exaltation or own house occupying Kendra

- When Moon in Cancer in the ascendant and any two are exalted out of four

- Out of four only one exalted in the ascendant

7.10 Vipreet Raj Yoga

This yoga is formed when planets ruling a dusthana house (6,8,12) occupy another dusthana.

Harsha yoga—The 6th lord is in the 8th or the 12th house

Sarala yoga-The 8th lord is in the 6th or 12th

Vimala yoga—The 12th lord is in the 6th or 8th

It is said to give sudden unexpected rise in life, usually after an initial setback or misfortune.

7.11 Saraswati Yoga

Saraswati Yoga forms when Jupiter, Venus, and Mercury occupy lagna, 2nd, 4th, 5th, 7th, 9th, or 10th house either jointly or separately and Jupiter is in its own sign, friend, or exalted sign. The person with this yoga in the horoscope will be highly intelligent and famous for his wisdom. He will be very proficient in composing prose, poetry, drama, and would be well versed in Shastra and Mathematics. He will be skilled in narrative composition and in the exposition of sacred texts.

7.12 Neecha-Bhanga Raja Yoga

This yoga indicates the cancellation of the debilitation of a planet. "Neech" means the planet is not powerful and is facing the conditions of lack of resources, "Bhanga" means that some other planet has come to help, and now the planet which is in the position of "Neech" enjoying now. The debilitated planet alone cannot do anything, but with the help of someone else, he is now able to achieve his desired task. A planet achieves Neecha-Bhanga when;

- The sign in which the debilitated planet is located, the planet which is exalted in that sign, should be in the Kendra from the Lagna or Moon.

- The lord of the house in which the planet is debilitated is in the Kendra from the Ascendant or Moon.

- The owner of the sign where the debilitated planet is exalted is situated with it.

- The debilitated planet is associated with or aspected by its exalted lord.

- The lord of the sign occupied by the debilitated planet aspects the debilitated planet.

- Debilitated planet is in exalted sign in Navamsa Kundli.

7.13 Lakshmi Yoga

Lakshmi yoga is formed when the lord of lagna is very powerful and strongly placed in its own sign or exaltation sign and it must also be in Kendra or trikona. The lord of the 9th house must be placed in either its own sign or exalted sign and it must be in Kendra or trikona house.

7.14 Parvata Yoga

This yoga is formed when benefics should be in posited in Kendras, and the 6th and 8th house must be free or occupied by benefics. This yoga is also formed when the lord of Lagna and the 12th should be in mutual kendras. This yoga indicates the person will be wealthy, liberal, charitable, and head of a town or village.

7.15 Sankha Yoga

This yoga is formed when the fifth lord and the sixth lord are in mutual kendras, and the lagna lord is strong. The native is kind-hearted, virtuous, learned, versed in sacred scriptures, and enjoys prosperity.

7.16 Srik Yoga (Maala) and Sarpa Yoga

If all the benefics occupy kendras and no malefics in kendra, Srik Yoga is caused. If all the malefics in kendras and no benefics in kendras, Sarpa yoga is caused.

The person born in Srik Yoga will live in comfort, will possess conveyance and will have many enjoyments. Sarpa Yoga renders one miserable in many ways, cruel and stupid.

7.17 Maha – Bhagaya Yoga

For Male and Female natives, the formation of this yoga has different criteria –

For the Male chart –

- Birth during daytime (between sunrise and sunset)

- Odd sign rising in the lagna

- The Sun occupying an odd sign, and

- The Moon is also in an odd sign

For Female Chart –

- Birth during nighttime (between sunset and sunrise)

- Even signs rising in the lagna

- The Sun occupying an even sign, and

- The Moon is also in an even sign

A man born under this yoga will be of good character, helpful, generous, famous, and will live in good old age. A woman born in this combination gets a long life, children, and wealth and is of good conduct.

7.18 Guru Chandal Yoga

Brihaspati is known as Guru in Sanskrit and Chandala means, mean or demon. When Rahu and Ketu conjunct with Jupiter in any house, then it is called Guru Chandal Yoga. The effect of Guru Chandal Dosha depends on the position of Jupiter and Rahu in different houses in different conditions. Due to this dosha, the native will find it difficult to achieve success and excel in education and career.

7.19 Vasumati Yoga

If the natural benefic planets like Jupiter, Venus, Mercury and Moon occupy Upachaya houses – 3rd, 6th, 10th & 11th either from the Ascendant or Moon, this powerful financial yoga is created.

If the planets are in exaltation in the Upachaya house, then this yoga becomes very powerful, whereas if the planets are in debilitation, then this yoga becomes weak.

7.20 Grahan Dosh

Grahan dosh takes place due to Rahu, Ketu, Sun, and Moon. When Sun or Moon is placed with Rahu or Ketu in a chart, then Grahan Dosh happens.

7.21 Kala Sarpa Dosh

When all the planets including Lagna are confined within Rahu and Ketu, it is known as Kaal Sarp Dosh or Kaal Sarp Yoga. If any planet is outside this Rahu-Ketu axis, then this Kaalsarp Yog will be broken and no harmful result of this Yoga will be experienced. Even if the Ascendant is outside this axis, this yoga will not be formed. According to the position of Rahu and Ketu in the birth chart, there are 12 types of Kaal Sarp Dosh.

1. Anant Kaal Sarp Dosh

2. Kulik Kaal Sarp Dosh

3. Vasuki Kaal Sarp Dosh

4. Shankhapal Kaal Sarp Dosh

5. Padam Kaal Sarp Dosh

6. Mahapadma Kaal Sarp Dosh

7. Takshak Kaal Sarp Dosh

8. Karkotak Kaal Sarp dosh

9. Shankhnaad Kaal Sarp Dosh

10. Ghatak Kaal Sarp Dosh

11. Vishdhar Kaal Sarp Dosh

12. Shashnaag Kaal Sarp Dosh

Chapter 8

Transit of Planets

A horoscope is a snapshot of the sky when a person is born, the zodiac signs that rise and set at the time and the planetary positions in them, guide the life path of the person. But the planets are not fixed, they keep on moving and transiting through different signs. This transit produces different types of energy. Although the effect of the transiting planet is temporary in our life and when the planet moves out of the zodiac, the energy level changes, and then its effect also changes.

We can understand the planets in the birth chart as mother and father, who always have an impact on us, no matter how old we become. The transiting planet is like our class teacher, when we study in class 1st then our class teacher has full right to punish us, but when we leave the class and study in higher classes, then the authority goes to that class teacher. Similarly, the transiting planet affects us as long as it remains in that sign. When it leaves and some other planet comes then the right to influence us goes to the newcomer. But what we got from our parents affects our whole life, in the same way, the planets of birth affect us throughout life.

Transit provides us with useful information about upcoming changes in energy levels and favorable and unfavorable times. The information guides us to channelize our energy in the right direction, make better use of available resources, and take necessary measures on gloomy days. This information also destroys the person's ego and despair, that there is higher energy working behind us. As a human we only have to do our work, which eliminates the attachment to the words "I did it". We have to sow only good seeds, fruits will come when the time turns favourable.

The effect of transits of slow-moving planets – Jupiter, Saturn, Rahu and Ketu are longer than that of fast-moving planets. Jupiter stays in a sign for almost a year, Saturn stays in a sign for 2.5 years, Rahu and Ketu stay in a sign for 1.5 years. Many life changing events take place during this transit which affects the person deeply.

Jupiter, Venus, unafflicted Mercury, and Moon (more than 72 degrees) are considered benefic planets. While transiting they produce favorable results when they conjoin or make aspects with the position of planets in our natal chart. Sun is considered kroora (cruel) and Mars, Saturn, Rahu, and Ketu are considered malefic and produce unfavorable results when they conjoin or make aspects with the planets in our horoscope. When a benefic planet transits in its favourable signs and conjoins or makes an aspect with a benefic planet then it produces favorable results and vice-versa.

Jupiter's most favorable sign is cancer, therefore, when Jupiter transit through cancer most favorable results is possible, while Saturn's most detrimental sign is also cancer, when Saturn transits into Cancer many life-changing events happen.

8.1 The Transit of Jupiter

Jupiter takes one year time to cross a sign and complete the entire zodiac in 12 years. Therefore, after every 12 years, Jupiter transit over its natal Jupiter, and that time brings remarkable changes in the life of the person. Jupiter is the most benefic planet, so its transit brings luck, happiness, and success in life. When Jupiter transits over the natal Moon or 7th house or makes an aspect then most of the native's marriages happen at that time. It bestows the person with children, wealth, and happy life. One of the most auspicious times comes when it transits the 2nd, 5th, 7th, 9th, and 11th houses from the natal Moon.

8.2 The Transit of Saturn

Saturn completes its cycle in 29.5 years and stays in a sign for 2.5 years. The tough master transit brings limitations, restrictions, delays, and misfortunes. When Saturn transits over the natal Sun, problems with the father, seniors, and authorities are possible. Saturn is the challenger, so subordinate will challenge their superiors and the transit creates a lot of trouble in the native's life.

Saturn's transit over Moon brings problems with mother, depression, and mental agony. Saturn transit over Venus brings trouble with the wife, female relatives, and scandals. There is also the possibility of financial gains during such a transit. Its transit over Mars brings quarrels and accidents, its transit over Jupiter brings financial gains and the start of a new venture, success in investments; its transit over Mercury brings trouble through documents, also increased interest in literature and study. Saturn's transit over natal Saturn brings significant changes in life and it put questions on everything that the person has done till now is his life.

Saturn means balance and discipline. The transit of Saturn teaches the person to be balanced, it destroys the ego of the person and shows the real truth of life.

8.3 The Transit of Rahu & Ketu

Rahu and Ketu always move retrograde and complete one cycle in 18 years and stay in a sign for 1.5 years. The behavior of both these nodes is sudden, so when they change their sign unexpected events happen. The event triggered by them can affect the native for 1.5 years as they stay in that zodiac during that period.

The shadow planet Rahu is considered a curtain. At our home curtain prevents the sunlight from coming into the room and the room becomes slightly darker. When Rahu transit over the natal Sun then the sunlight becomes dim or when Rahu comes in front of the natal Sun then it works as a curtain and prevents Sunlight from coming into that house. Due to the absence of sunlight, the problem related to the house starts which can last for 1.5 years.

After every 18 years, these two nodes return to the same position in the natal chart, then many significant changes happen in the life of the person. Rahu represents hunger and Ketu represents separation. These two nodes represent disturbed energies, where the nodes are placed the matter related to the house is always disturbed. The house in which, they are located in the birth chart, after 18 years when they return over there, the energy level would become high and unexpected events may happen related to the house concerned.

Chapter 9

Vimshottari Dasha System

Dasha means the period, astrology considers it a certain time ruled by a planet. As time changes the ruling planet changes and dasha changes. Sage Parashara has considered the natural lifespan of a person to be 120 years and states that among many types of dasha systems, Vimshottari is the most appropriate for the general populace. Dasha system works on the basis of Nakshatra. The time is always running under certain dasha, but it is different for every person. Sage Parashara has described the dasha period of all nine planets; Ketu 7 years, Venus 20 years, Sun 6 years, Moon 10, Mars 7 years, Rahu 18 years, Jupiter 16 years, Saturn 19 years, and Mercury 17 years.

The Nakshatra in which the Moon is at the time of the birth of the person is known as "Janma Nakshatra". The lord of that

Nakshatra is considered to start the Mahadasha of the native and the rest of the period follows the order described by Sage Parashara. Suppose, at the time of the birth Moon is in Kritika nakshatra, and the lord of Kritika is the Sun, therefore, the first Mahadasha of the native starts from the Sun, and thereafter Moon, Mars, etc. The following table presents the relationship between; 27 nakshatra, lords, and its period.

Nakshatra			Lords	Years Allocated - Vimshottari
Ashwini	Magha	Mula	Ketu	7
Bharani	P. Phalguni	P. Ashadha	Venus	20
Krttika	U. Phalguni	U. Ashadha	Sun	6
Rohini	Hasta	Shravana	Moon	10
Mrigashirsha	Chitra	Dhanishta	Mars	7
Ardra	Swati	Satabhisha	Rahu	18
Punarvasu	Vishakha	P. Bhadrapada	Jupiter	16
Pushya	Anuradha	U. Bhadrapada	Saturn	19
Aslesha	Jyeshtha	Revati	Mercury	17
			TOTAL	**120**

(Note: P. - Puvra; U. - Uttara)

The sub-division of the dasha system is as follows:

1) Mahadasha	4) Sookshma Dasha
2) Antardasha	5) Praanadasha
3) Pratyantar Dasha	6) Dehadasha

Mahadasha, and Antardasha (which is also known as Bhukti) are the important divisions of the dasha system. The relationship between the lord of the Mahadasha and the lord of the Antardasha is very crucial as it affects the outcome of the life of the native. If the relationship between these two is good then time will be favorable for the person and he enjoys the fruits of his efforts, but if the relationship between these two is not good then there will be obstacles. Though the final decision will be taken by the Mahadasha lord, the decision of the Antardasha lord also matters as the Bhukti period gives you the accurate timing calculation of the event.

When the Mahadasha changes, the dominance changes. The energy which was affecting the person for a long time now starts changing and the new energy starts affecting the person. In such a situation, the life of a person is not as normal as before. Like a new ruler comes and an old ruler goes. This is the time of transition of energies for 2 to 3 months. Soon everything is set up as per the order of the lord of the new Mahadasha.

Chapter 10

Ashktakvarga

'Ashta' means eight, and 'Varga' means classification, hence, the word Ashtakvarga means eight types of classifications. The classification is a combination of seven planets and lagna, these combinations create eight different types of energies which can be benefic or malefic and depend on the position of the planets. Maharishi Parashara introduced this concept in his book 'Brihat Parashara Hora Shastra' and it is a unique system of prediction in Hindu Astrology without which prediction is totally impossible.

10.1 Basic Concept

There are total nine planets considered in Hindu Astrology, but the Ashtakvarga system considers only seven planets and leaves Rahu and Ketu, with lagna there are eight in number. Therefore, there are eight types of energies that every planet release and these can be good or bad. The release of benefic energy is called 'Bindus' (Dots) and the release of malefic energy is called 'Rekhas' (Small lines).

10.2 Tables in Ashktakvarga

- **Bhinnashtakvarga** – This table considers only seven planets (leaving Rahu and Ketu).

- **Saravashtakvarga or Samudayashatakvarga** – This table represents the sum of total bindus in each house received by a planet from eight different sources.

- **Prastarashtak Varga** – This table represents a complete picture of Ashtakvarga in 12 signs.

10.3 Bhinnashtakvarga

The auspicious places of the planets with respect to themselves and the seven other planets including the Ascendant are as follows:

The Sun									
Benefic Places									**Total**
Sun	1	2	4	7	8	9	10	11	8
Moon	3	6	10	11					4
Mars	1	2	4	7	8	9	10	11	8
Mercury	3	5	6	9	10	11	12		7
Jupiter	5	6	9	11					4
Venus	6	7	12						3
Saturn	1	2	4	7	8	9	10	11	8
Lagna	3	4	6	10	11	12			6
									48

The Moon									
Benefic Places									**Total**
Sun	3	6	7	8	10	11			6
Moon	1	3	6	7	10	11			6
Mars	2	3	5	6	9	10	11		7
Mercury	1	3	4	5	7	8	10	11	8
Jupiter	1	4	7	8	10	11	12		7
Venus	3	4	5	7	9	10	11		7
Saturn	3	5	6	11					4
Lagna	3	6	10	11					4
									49

<table>
<tr><td colspan="9" align="center">Mars</td></tr>
<tr><td colspan="8" align="center">Benefic Places</td><td>Total</td></tr>
<tr><td>Sun</td><td>3</td><td>5</td><td>6</td><td>10</td><td>11</td><td></td><td></td><td>5</td></tr>
<tr><td>Moon</td><td>3</td><td>6</td><td>11</td><td></td><td></td><td></td><td></td><td>3</td></tr>
<tr><td>Mars</td><td>1</td><td>2</td><td>4</td><td>7</td><td>8</td><td>10</td><td>11</td><td>7</td></tr>
<tr><td>Mercury</td><td>3</td><td>5</td><td>6</td><td>11</td><td></td><td></td><td></td><td>4</td></tr>
<tr><td>Jupiter</td><td>6</td><td>10</td><td>11</td><td>12</td><td></td><td></td><td></td><td>4</td></tr>
<tr><td>Venus</td><td>6</td><td>8</td><td>11</td><td>12</td><td></td><td></td><td></td><td>4</td></tr>
<tr><td>Saturn</td><td>1</td><td>4</td><td>7</td><td>8</td><td>9</td><td>10</td><td>11</td><td>7</td></tr>
<tr><td>Lagna</td><td>1</td><td>3</td><td>6</td><td>10</td><td>11</td><td></td><td></td><td>5</td></tr>
<tr><td colspan="8"></td><td>39</td></tr>
</table>

<table>
<tr><td colspan="10" align="center">Mercury</td></tr>
<tr><td colspan="9" align="center">Benefic Places</td><td>Total</td></tr>
<tr><td>Sun</td><td>5</td><td>6</td><td>9</td><td>11</td><td>12</td><td></td><td></td><td></td><td>5</td></tr>
<tr><td>Moon</td><td>2</td><td>4</td><td>6</td><td>8</td><td>10</td><td>11</td><td></td><td></td><td>6</td></tr>
<tr><td>Mars</td><td>1</td><td>2</td><td>4</td><td>7</td><td>8</td><td>9</td><td>10</td><td>11</td><td>8</td></tr>
<tr><td>Mercury</td><td>1</td><td>3</td><td>5</td><td>6</td><td>9</td><td>10</td><td>11</td><td>12</td><td>8</td></tr>
<tr><td>Jupiter</td><td>6</td><td>8</td><td>11</td><td>12</td><td></td><td></td><td></td><td></td><td>4</td></tr>
<tr><td>Venus</td><td>1</td><td>2</td><td>3</td><td>4</td><td>5</td><td>8</td><td>9</td><td>11</td><td>8</td></tr>
<tr><td>Saturn</td><td>1</td><td>2</td><td>4</td><td>7</td><td>8</td><td>9</td><td>10</td><td>11</td><td>8</td></tr>
<tr><td>Lagna</td><td>1</td><td>2</td><td>4</td><td>6</td><td>8</td><td>10</td><td>11</td><td></td><td>7</td></tr>
<tr><td colspan="9"></td><td>54</td></tr>
</table>

Jupiter										Total
Benefic Places										**Total**
Sun	1	2	3	4	7	8	9	10	11	9
Moon	2	5	7	9	11					5
Mars	1	2	4	7	8	10	11			7
Mercury	1	2	4	5	6	9	10	11		8
Jupiter	1	2	3	4	7	8	10	11		8
Venus	2	5	6	9	10	11				6
Saturn	3	5	6	12						4
Lagna	1	2	4	5	6	7	9	10	11	9
										56

Venus										Total
Benefic Places										**Total**
Sun	8	11	12							3
Moon	1	2	3	4	5	8	9	11	12	9
Mars	3	5	6	9	11	12				6
Mercury	3	5	6	9	11					5
Jupiter	5	8	9	10	11					5
Venus	1	2	3	4	5	8	9	10	11	9
Saturn	3	4	5	8	9	10	11			7
Lagna	1	2	3	4	5	8	9	11		8
										52

Saturn							
Benefic Places							**Total**
Sun	1	2	4	7	8	10	11	7
Moon	3	6	11					3
Mars	3	5	6	10	11	12		6
Mercury	6	8	9	10	11	12		6
Jupiter	5	6	11	12				4
Venus	6	11	12					3
Saturn	3	5	6	11				4
Lagna	1	3	4	6	10	11		6
								39

10.4 Interpretation of Ashtakvarga Table

In the table, we need to observe the total number of bindus obtained by the planet and the total bindus in the sign. The maximum number of bindus in a sign is 8, if a planet has 4 bindus then the result would be mediocre to good, more than 5 to 8 is very good to excellent.

Sun: On the scale of 8 bindus, the transit of the Sun would be considered strong if it obtained more than 5 binus in a sign. An excellent result would be possible when more bindus is obtained, 4 is considered as average, and less than 4 means inauspicious results likely to be possible.

Moon: If bindus are 5 or more then the transit bestows the person with favourable results, 4 is considered average, 1 to 3 indicates pessimism are 0 means melancholic state of mind.

Mars: Up to 3 bindus, Mars is considered weak and leads to quarrels, pessimism, loss of status and wealth. 4 bindus gives average results while 5 to 8 bindus are excellent.

Mercury: 4 bindus are average, 5 to 8 are excellent and 0 to 3 are poor. Weak Mercury in 6th or 8th houses with poor bindus – the person becomes unreliable and crooked in behavior.

Jupiter: 4 bindus are average, 5 to 8 are excellent, success, gain of wealth, and 0 to 3 are poor. A weak Jupiter with poor bindus, life will become unfortunate and full of struggles.

Venus: 4 bindus are average, 5 to 8 are excellent and 0 to 3 are poor. Weak Venus causes marital problems, poverty, scandals, and life without meaning.

Saturn: 4 bindus are average, 5 to 8 are excellent and 0 to 3 are poor. Weak Saturn causes hindrances, delays, sickness, death, disease, and poverty.

10.5 Sarvashtakvarga

The total points in the Sarvashtakvarga table are 337. These points are divided into 12 bhavas, divide 337 into 12, 28 is the average point for each bhava. However, the minimum number of points is different for each bhava, but 28 is considered as strong. If a bhava has more than 28 points then it is considered a strong bhava and able to generate auspicious results. As the numbers are higher the result would be much better, transit of planets over these bhavas able to produce favourable results. The points below 28 are considered as weak bhava, if the count falls below 21 then it is inauspicious, a lower number means to struggle and problems and transit of the planet may produce adverse results.

The minimum number of bindus for each bhava is:

Houses	Bindus
Lagna	25
2nd House	22
3rd House	29
4th House	24
5th House	25
6th House	34

Houses	Bindus
7th House	19
8th House	24
9th House	29
10th House	36
11th House	54
12th House	16

Lagna - Lagna represents the self, the points in this bhava indicate the confidence of the person. The points here more than 28 indicate the courageous nature of the person, such type of person does not feel panic in adverse circumstances. Less than 25 points indicate a lack of courage and less than 21 means coward person.

2nd House - More points in the second house indicate enough savings for the person.

3rd House - It is the house of courage; more points indicate brave nature while fewer points indicate dependency and lack of initiative.

4th House - It is the house of home, comfort, and early education. Points in this house more than 24 indicate smooth education, and comfort at home, while fewer points indicate problems in education and lack of resources.

5th House - It is the house of creation, interest, and children. Fewer points mean difficulty in getting children, the person faces extreme difficulties to fulfill his dreams.

6th House - This is the house of immunity. More points indicate strong immunity of the person, while fewer points mean easily vulnerable to diseases.

7th House – This is the house of spouse and partnership. More points mean good relations with spouse, if points are below 15 indicates a problem with spouse and partners.

8th House - This is the house of longevity. Fewer points do not mean less longevity but a depressed state of mind where a person lacks the necessary vitality and vigour in his life.

9th House – This is the house of religion and higher education. Fewer points indicate the person has no belief in religion and may face problems in getting higher education.

10th House – More points indicate the person is responsible for his duties while fewer points indicate careless nature.

11th House – More points indicate higher income with less work, while fewer points indicate struggle in getting income.

12th House – This is the house of expenditure, so fewer points are good, more points indicate a spendthrift person. Very less points mean a miser person.

Chapter 11

Basics of Nakshatras

Vedic astrology considers the influence of 27 constellations on the earth. It has divided the entire zodiac into 27 parts, thus each nakshatra is 13 degrees 20 minutes. Also, the duration of 13 degrees 20 minutes is divided into 4 parts, each part called pada which spans 3 degrees 20 minutes. Moon takes 27.3 days to complete one revolution and stays for one day in one constellation. In other words, the average daily motion of the Moon is 13.2 degrees. In Hindu mythology, these 27 constellations are the 27 wives of the Moon.

These nakshatras and their pada define the characteristics of the planets placed in them. They decide the person's traits, characteristics, thinking patterns, likes, dislikes, etc. One of the nine planets is considered to be the lord of that nakshatra and each nakshatra has its own Deity. Deities and Nakshatra lords have a profound effect on a person and their inherent characteristics lie within that person. The lord of the pada plays an important role as the characteristics of the pada lord also deeply affect the person.

Suppose, a person is born when the Moon was in the fourth pada of Chitra Nakshatra. The third and fourth pada of Chitra Nakshatra belongs to Libra and its lord is Venus, Chitra constellation lord is Mars and the fourth pada lord is also Mars, and the deity of Chitra is "Tavastar- the celestial architect – Vishwakarma". So, such a person will reflect the qualities of Venus-Mars-Mars and will also have the characteristics of Vishwakarma. Our sages have given many other qualities of constellations, some of them are listed in the table below.

11.1 Nakshatra, Zodiac Position and Lord

Sr. No.		Nakshatra	Zodiac	Nakshatra Lord
1		Ashwini	0° – 13°20′ Mesha	Ketu
2		Bharani	13° 20′ – 26°40′ Mesha	Venus
3		Krttika	26°40′ Mesha – 10° Vrishabha	Sun
4	**Rajasic**	Rohini	10° – 23°20′ Vrishabha	Moon
5		Mrigashirsha	23° 20′ Vrishabha – 6° 40′ Mithuna	Mars
6		Ardra	6° 40′ – 20° Mithuna	Rahu
7		Punarvasu	20° Mithuna – 3°20′ Karka	Jupiter
8		Pushya	3°20′ -16°40′ Karka	Saturn
9		Aslesha	16°40′ – 30° Karka	Mercury
10		Magha	0° – 13°20′ Simha	Ketu
11		P. Phalguni	13°20′ – 26°40′ Simha	Venus
12		U. Phalguni	26°40′ Simha- 10° Kanya	Sun
13	**Tamasic**	Hasta	10° – 23°20′ Kanya	Moon
14		Chitra	23°20′ Kanya – 6°40′ Tula	Mars
15		Swati	6°40′ – 20° Tula	Rahu
16		Vishakha	20° Tula – 3°20′ Vrishchika	Jupiter
17		Anuradha	3°20′ – 16°40′ Vrishchika	Saturn
18		Jyeshtha	16°40′ – 30° Vrishchika	Mercury
19		Mula	0° – 13°20′ Dhanu	Ketu
20		P. Ashadha	13°20′ – 26°40′ Dhanu	Venus
21		U. Ashadha	26°40′ Dhanu – 10° Makara	Sun
22	**Satwic**	Shravana	10° – 23°20′ Makara	Moon
23		Dhanishta	23°20′ Makara – 6°40′ Kumbha	Mars
24		Satabhisha	6°40′ – 20° Kumbha	Rahu
25		P. Bhadrapada	20° Kumbha – 3°20′ Meena	Jupiter
26		U. Bhadrapada	3°20′ – 16°40′ Meena	Saturn
27		Revati	16°40′ – 30° Meena	Mercury

11.2 Nakshatra, Deity and Symbol

Sr. No.	Nakshatra	Deity	Symbol
1	Ashwini	Ashvini Kumaras	Horse head
2	Bharani	Yama	Vagina
3	Krittika	Agni	Axe, sharp edge
4	Rohini	Prajapati - Lord of creation	Chariot
5	Mrigashirsha	Soma - God of immortality	Head of a deer
6	Ardra	Rudra - The Lord of Storms	Teardrop, Diamond
7	Punarvasu	Aditi - the universal mother	Quiver of arrows
8	Pushya	Brihaspati	Milk yielding by the teat of a cow
9	Aslesha	Naga	Coiled snake
10	Magha	The Pitris - The Ancestral Fathers	Throne
11	P. Phalguni	Bhaga - God of love and marriage	Hammock, front legs of bed
12	U. Phalguni	Aryama - God of vows and	Bed, legs of a cot
13	Hasta	Savitar - God of sunrise	Hand or fist
14	Chitra	Tvastar - Vishwakarma	Multifaceted jewel
15	Swati	Vayu-Wind	Sword, coral
16	Vishakha	Indragni- Gods of lightning and	Potter's wheel
17	Anuradha	Mitra - the God of friendship	Lotus flower
18	Jyeshtha	Indra	Umbrella, Earring
19	Mula	Nirritti – Alaksmi	Bunch of roots tied together
20	P. Ashadha	Apas - goddess of Waters	Tusk of an elephant - left, Fan
21	U. Ashadha	Vishvadevas-Universal Gods	Tusk of an elephant - right
22	Shravana	Vishnu	Three footprints, trident, ear
23	Dhanishta	The eight Vasus	Musical drum
24	Satabhisha	Varuna	Empty circle or a charm
25	P. Bhadrapada	Aja Ekapada - Unicorn	Front of a funeral cot, Two faced man
26	U. Bhadrapada	Ahir Budhya	Back legs of a funeral cot
27	Revati	Pushan – The Nurturer	Fish swimming in the water, Drum

11.3 Nakshatra and Pada Lord

Nakshatra	Nakshatra Lord	Pada 1	Pada 2	Pada 3	Pada 4
Ashwini	Ketu	Mar	Ven	Mer	Mo
Bharani	Venus	Sun	Mer	Ven	Mar
Krttika	Sun	Jup	Sat	Sat	Jup
Rohini	Moon	Mar	Ven	Mer	Mo
Mrigashirsha	Mars	Sun	Mer	Ven	Mar
Ardra	Rahu	Jup	Sat	Sat	Jup
Punarvasu	Jupiter	Mar	Ven	Mer	Mo
Pushya	Saturn	Sun	Mer	Ven	Mar
Aslesha	Mercury	Jup	Sat	Sat	Jup
Magha	Ketu	Mar	Ven	Mer	Mo
Purva phalguni	Venus	Sun	Mer	Ven	Mar
Uttara phalguni	Sun	Jup	Sat	Sat	Jup
Hasta	Moon	Mar	Ven	Mer	Mo
Chitra	Mars	Sun	Mer	Ven	Mar
Swati	Rahu	Jup	Sat	Sat	Jup
Vishakha	Jupiter	Mar	Ven	Mer	Mo
Anuradha	Saturn	Sun	Mer	Ven	Mar
Jyeshtha	Mercury	Jup	Sat	Sat	Jup
Mula	Ketu	Mar	Ven	Mer	Mo
Purva ashadha	Venus	Sun	Mer	Ven	Mar
Uttara ashadha	Sun	Jup	Sat	Sat	Jup
Shravana	Moon	Mar	Ven	Mer	Mo
Dhanishta	Mars	Sun	Mer	Ven	Mar
Satabhisha	Rahu	Jup	Sat	Sat	Jup
Purva bhadrapada	Jupiter	Mar	Ven	Mer	Mo
Uttara bhadrapada	Saturn	Sun	Mer	Ven	Mar
Revati	Mercury	Jup	Sat	Sat	Jup

11.4 Nature of Nakshatra

Light	Mridu (Soft)	Mixed (Sharp+Soft)	Dhruva (Fixed)	Ugra (Dreadful)	Tikshna (Sharp)	Chara (Movable)
Ashvini	Mrigashirsha	Krttika	Rohini	Bharani	Ardra	Punarvasu
Pushya	Chitra	Vishakha	Uttara phalguni	Magha	Aslesha	Swati
Hasta	Anuradha		Uttara ashadha	Purva phalguni	Jyeshtha	Dhanishta
	Revati		Shravana	Purva ashadha	Mula	Satabhisha
			Uttara bhadrapada	Purva bhadrapada		

11.5 Animal Symbol and Inimical Yoni

Male	Female	Animal Symbol	Inimical
Ashiwini	Satabhisha	Horse	Buffalo
Bharni	Revati	Elephant	Lion
Pushya	Kritika	Sheep (Goat)	Monkey
Rohini	Mrigashirsha	Serpent	Mongoose
Mula	Ardra	Dog	Deer
Aslesha	Punarvasu	Cat	Rat
Magha	Purva phalguni	Rat	Cat
Uttara phalguni	Uttara bhadrapada	Bull / Cow	Tiger
Swati	Hasta	Buffalo	Horse
Vishakha	Chitra	Tiger	Cow
Jyeshtha	Anuradha	Deer (Hare)	Dog
Purva ashadha	Shravana	Monkey	Sheep
Purva bhadrapada	Dhanishta	Lion	Elephant
Uttara ashadha		Mongoose	Serpent

11.6 Caste

Brahmin	Kshatriya	Vaishya	Shudra	Mleccha/ Outcaste	Servant	Butcher
Krttika	Pushya	Ashwini	Rohini	Bharani	Mrigashirsha	Ardra
Purva phalguni	Uttara phalguni	Punarvasu	Magha	Aslesha	Chitra	Swati
Purva ashadha	Uttara ashadha	Hasta	Anuradha	Vishakha	Jyeshtha	Mula
Purva bhadrapada	Uttara bhadrapada		Revati	Shravana	Dhanishta	Satabhisha

11.7 Marraige

Auspicious	Not auspicious
Rohini	Ashwini
Magha	Bharani
Purva phalguni	Krttika
Uttara phalguni	Mrigashirsha
Hasta	Ardra
Swati	Punarvasu
Uttara ashadha	Pushya
Uttara bhadrapada	Aslesha
Revati	Chitra
	Vishakha
	Anuradha
	Jyeshtha
	Mula
	Purva ashadha
	Shravana
	Dhanishta
	Satabhisha
	Purva bhadrapada

11.8 Direction

Upward	Downward	Sideways
Rohini	Bharani	Ashwini
Ardra	Krttika	Mrigashirsha
Pushya	Aslesha	Punarvasu
Purva phalguni	Magha	Hasta
Uttara ashadha	Uttara phalguni	Chitra
Shravana	Vishakha	Swati
Dhanishta	Mula	Anuradha
Satabhisha	Purva ashadha	Jyeshtha
Uttara bhadrapada	Purva bhadrapada	Revati

11.9 Activity

Active	Passive	Balanced
Krttika	Ashwini	Bharani
Aslesha	Mrigashirsha	Rohini
Magha	Punarvasu	Ardra
Chitra	Pushya	Purva phalguni
Vishakha	Hasta	Uttara phalguni
Jyeshtha	Swati	Purva ashadha
Mula	Anuradha	Uttara ashadha
Dhanishta	Shravana	Purva bhadrapada
Satabhisha		Uttara bhadrapada
		Revati

11.10 TriMurti

Brahma	Vishnu	Shiva
Ashwini	Bharani	Krttika
Rohini	Mrigashirsha	Ardra
Punarvasu	Pushya	Aslesha
Magha	Purva phalguni	Uttara phalguni
Hasta	Chitra	Swati
Vishakha	Anuradha	Jyeshtha
Mula	Purva ashadha	Uttara ashadha
Shravana	Dhanishta	Satabhisha
Purva bhadrapada	Uttara bhadrapada	Revati

(Note: Brahma - Creation, Vishnu - Maintenance, Shiva - Dissolution)

11.11 Gana

Dev	Manusha	Rakshasa
Ashwini	Bharani	Krttika
Mrigashirsha	Rohini	Aslesha
Punarvasu	Ardra	Magha
Pushya	Purva phalguni	Chitra
Hasta	Uttara phalguni	Vishakha
Swati	Purva ashadha	Jyeshtha
Anuradha	Uttara ashadha	Mula
Shravana	Purva bhadrapada	Dhanishta
Revati	Uttara bhadrapada	Satabhisha

11.12 Guna

Sr. No.	Nakshatra	Guna (Level 1)	Guna (Level 2)	Guna (Level 3)	Guna (Combined)
1	Ashwini	Rajasic	Rajasic	Rajasic	Rajasic-Rajasic-Rajasic
2	Bharani	Rajasic	Rajasic	Tamasic	Rajasic-Rajasic-Tamasic
3	Krttika	Rajasic	Rajasic	Satwic	Rajasic-Rajasic-Satwic
4	Rohini	Rajasic	Tamasic	Rajasic	Rajasic-Tamasic-Rajasic
5	Mrigashirsha	Rajasic	Tamasic	Tamasic	Rajasic-Tamasic-Tamasic
6	Ardra	Rajasic	Tamasic	Satwic	Rajasic-Tamasic-Satwic
7	Punarvasu	Rajasic	Satwic	Rajasic	Rajasic-Satwic-Rajasic
8	Pushya	Rajasic	Satwic	Tamasic	Rajasic-Satwic-Tamasic
9	Aslesha	Rajasic	Satwic	Satwic	Rajasic-Satwic-Satwic
10	Magha	Tamasic	Rajasic	Rajasic	Tamasic-Rajasic-Rajasic
11	Purva phalguni	Tamasic	Rajasic	Tamasic	Tamasic-Rajasic-Tamasic
12	Uttara phalguni	Tamasic	Rajasic	Satwic	Tamasic-Rajasic-Satwic
13	Hasta	Tamasic	Tamasic	Rajasic	Tamasic-Tamasic-Rajasic
14	Chitra	Tamasic	Tamasic	Tamasic	Tamasic-Tamasic-Tamasic
15	Swati	Tamasic	Tamasic	Satwic	Tamasic-Tamasic-Satwic
16	Vishakha	Tamasic	Satwic	Rajasic	Tamasic-Satwic-Rajasic
17	Anuradha	Tamasic	Satwic	Tamasic	Tamasic-Satwic-Tamasic
18	Jyeshtha	Tamasic	Satwic	Satwic	Tamasic-Satwic-Satwic
19	Mula	Satwic	Rajasic	Rajasic	Satwic-Rajasic-Rajasic
20	Purva ashadha	Satwic	Rajasic	Tamasic	Satwic-Rajasic-Tamasic
21	Uttara ashadha	Satwic	Rajasic	Satwic	Satwic-Rajasic-Satwic
22	Shravana	Satwic	Tamasic	Rajasic	Satwic-Tamasic-Rajasic
23	Dhanishta	Satwic	Tamasic	Tamasic	Satwic-Tamasic-Tamasic
24	Satabhisha	Satwic	Tamasic	Satwic	Satwic-Tamasic-Satwic
25	Purva bhadrapada	Satwic	Satwic	Rajasic	Satwic-Satwic-Rajasic
26	Uttara bhadrapada	Satwic	Satwic	Tamasic	Satwic-Satwic-Tamasic
27	Revati	Satwic	Satwic	Satwic	Satwic-Satwic-Satwic

11.13 Gender

Male	Female	Neuter
Ashwini	Bharani	Mrigashirsha
Pushya	Krttika	Mula
Punarvasu	Rohini	Satabhisha
Hasta	Ardra	
Anuradha	Aslesha	
Shravana	Magha	
Purva bhadrapada	Purva phalguni	
Uttara bhadrapada	Uttara phalguni	
	Chitra	
	Swati	
	Vishakha	
	Jyeshtha	
	Purva ashadha	
	Uttara ashadha	
	Dhanishta	
	Revati	

(Note- For a detailed analysis of the 27 nakshatras, readers can refer to my book "The Light of Nakshatras".)

Chapter 12

Planets and Profession

Selection of a career in today's world is very important, people wander here and there to find a suitable career. Information about the ruling planet can help a lot to find the natural inclination of the person. Along with ascendant 2nd, 6th and 10th houses and their lord play an important role in career selection. 2nd, 6th, and 10th are earthy sign which represents materialism. There is a relation between our savings (2nd house), our day-to-day life (6th house), and our karma (10th house). Hence, the triangle of earthy houses and the placement of their lord is necessary to observe. Among them 10th house and its lord are extremely important, it is the house of karma and the chief indicator of one's career and profession.

Moon rules our mind, hence the position of the Moon and the 10th house from the Moon is also important to consider. Navamsha chart is necessary to analyze and the position of 10th lord in Navamsha is taken into consideration. The planet that is more powerful among them will rule the career of the native.

12.1 Career by Planets

The Sun: The Sun is the king of the solar system; it represents government and authority. A strong Sun in a horoscope indicates a government job and authoritative position. It indicates success in subjects and professions related to Physics, Statistics, Mathematics, Political Science, Astronomy, Ayurveda, Medicine, Electricity, Business given by father, Bureaucrats, Administrative jobs, Presidents, Politicians, CEOs, Magistrates, Rulers, Jewelers, Goldsmith, Financier, etc.

The Moon: The Moon indicates profession related to the Shipping industry, Navy, Water department, Milk and other liquids, Jobs related to fruits and vegetables, Nurturing and helping jobs, Tour & Travel, Air hostess, Liquor, Cloth, Herbs, Caterers, Chemicals, Medical field, Para-Medical staff, Laundry, Fine arts, Music, Dance, Pharmacy, Bio-Chemistry, Environmental sciences, Agriculture, Navy, Journalism, Advertising, Hospitals, Plants, Nursery, Marine, Sailor, etc.

Mars: Mars indicates weapons of all kinds and is considered the lord of war. It indicates any job related to these fields like; Military and police departments. Any type of job involving small or large metal tools such as; Dentist, Engineering job, Hunter, Butcher, Barber, etc. Mars gives success in subjects and professions related to; Metals, Surgeons, Arms and ammunitions, Explosives, Fireworks, Furnaces, Athletes, Butchers, Gyms, Wrestling, Mechanics, Cooks, Blacksmiths, Property, Geology, Adventurous sports, etc.

Mercury: Mercury indicates professions related to; Accounts, Commerce, Insurance, Investments, Banks, Money, Publishing, Books, Journalism, Treasury, Telecommunication, Transportation, Trading, Broking, Astrology, Chartered Accountants, Journalism, Writer, Publisher, Teacher, Mathematics, Media, Web designing, Secretary, Clerk, Broker, Public relations, Messenger, Interpreter, Procession related to communication of any kind, Diplomats, Negotiators, Courier Services, Stenographer, Booksellers, Architect, Reporter, Merchandise, etc.

Jupiter: Jupiter gives success in subjects and professions related to Philosophy, Psychology, Vedas, Counselor, Financial Advisor, Bankers, Law, Treasury, Literature, Judge, Lawyer, Editor, Professor, Teachers, Management, Directors, Priest, Astrologer, Administrator, Minister, Head of the department, Spokesperson, Cashiers, Scholars, Religious heads, Preachers, Priests, Vice-chancellors, Lecturers, Professional Experts, Judges, Advocates, etc.

Venus: Venus gives success in subjects and professions related to Music, Dance, Arts, Poetry, Painting, Entertainment, Media, Theatres, Interior designer, Fashion Designer, Actor, Singer, Model, Cosmetics, Textiles, Garments, Perfumes, Beauty-parlor, Stage performer, Furniture, Cartoonist, Personal Secretory, Receptionists, Florists, Handicrafts, Weaving, Sociology, Architect, Photographer, Gemstones, Web development, Animation, Advertisement, Hotel Management, Business relating to females, Catering, Receptionist, Private secretary, Salesperson, Counsellors, Party organizers and marriage-related work, Stage show, Actor, Comedian, Beauty parlour, Photography, Chemical, Sculpture, etc.

Saturn: Saturn gives success in subjects and professions related to Oil & Gas, Iron & Steel, Metals & Mines, Real estate, Law, Labour & Servants, Municipality workers, Agriculture, Head of a labor union, Coffin maker, Cremation ground, Ice-maker, Cold storage, Preservatives, Geography, Archeology, Bricks, Tiles, Stones, Leather goods, Machines, Workshop, Wool, Quarries, etc.

Rahu: Rahu gives success in subjects and professions related to Poison, Medicines made from poison, Homeopathy, Researchers of medicine or drugs, Waste- material-dealers, Cosmetic surgeon, Smokes, Mobile, Technology, Environmental Science, Lawyer, Airlines, Sweepers, Detective, Magician, Anesthetist, Aeronautical Engineering, Astronomers, Wine sellers, Politics, Diplomacy, Speculation, Television, Innovation, and all non-conventional careers, Import-Export, etc.

Ketu: Ketu gives success in subjects and professions related to Computers, Programming Language, Microbiologist, Saints, Detective, Secret affairs, Knowledgeable in the cryptic genre, Philosophy, Religion doctrines, Self-analysis, Occult, Palmists, Chemist, Preacher, Metaphysics Import-Export, etc.

12.2 Career by Signs

Aries: Military, Police, Surgeon, Firefighting, Athletes, Entrepreneur, etc.

Taurus: Music, Cosmetics, Luxury goods, Jewelry, Fashion, Money management, Teaching, Agriculture, Hospitality, etc.

Gemini: Media, Journalism, Public relations, Marketing, Broadcaster, Advertising, Accountants, Sales person, Translators, Writers, etc.

Cancer: Marine, Nursing, Hospitality, Human resources, Interior designing, Food, Restaurant, Home care, Child care, Personal secretary, Sailors, etc.

Leo: Corporate executive, Government jobs, Politics, Financial services, Investing, Speaker, etc.

Virgo: Accountant, Technician, Data scientists, Astrology, Media, Medical, Proof reader, Editor, Detective, Administrator, Forensic technician, Survey, Research work, etc.

Libra: Art, Dance, Architecture, Judges, Cosmetics, Fashion, Receptionists, Advertising, Interior decorating, Prostitutes, etc.

Scorpio: Chemicals, Drugs, Liquids, Insurance, Medical, Therapist, Detective, Body-guard, Investigator, Occult, Police, Research, etc.

Sagittarius: Religion, Banking and finance, Entrepreneurs, Sportsperson, Tour guide, Philanthropist, Correspondent, Coach, etc.

Capricorn: Logistics, Supply chain, Agent, Career Counsellor, Financial advisor, Administrator, etc.

Aquarius: Scientists, Inventors, Musicians, Designers, Consultants, Philosophers, Engineers, Computing, etc.

Pisces: Doctors, Nurses, Hospitals, Marine related, Charity worker, Film director, Counselors, Prisons, etc.

12.3 Career by Houses

First House: Self-employment, The body (gym), etc.

Second House: Banking, Investments, Finance, Teaching, Accountants, Food-related business, etc.

Third House: Communication, Writing, Publishing, Sales, Advertising, Travel, Import-export, etc.

Fourth House: Education, Agriculture, Vehicle, Real estate, Water, Mining, etc.

Fifth House: Speculation, Stock brokers, Entertainment, Creation, Self-expression, etc.

Sixth House: Health, Fitness, Labour, Police, Court, Loan recovery, Clinics, etc.

Seventh House: Partnership in business, Females, Foreign business, etc.

Eighth House: Insurance, Research, Secret, Occult, Sex, Cremation, etc.

Ninth House: University, Higher education, Religion, Teaching, Long travel, Head of the temple, etc.

Tenth House: Public life, etc.

Eleventh House: Group work, Side ventures, etc.

Twelfth House: Foreign, Hospitals, Prisons, Charities, etc.

Chapter 13

Weak Planets & Remedies

The **Sun**: When the Sun is weak in a horoscope the native has low self-confidence, is unable to go ahead alone, and always seeks dependency, the problem with the boss, lack of support with father or relation with father is not good, problem in eyes, frustrate very easily and feel depressed, suffer from an inferiority complex, unable to digest the word "No", bone-related problem, tries to hide himself and less socializes, suffer from frequent headaches, always feeling insecure and seeking safety first.

Remedies for the Sun:

- Chant Aditya Hridaya Stotra daily

- Chant Chakshushopanishad for problems related to eyes

- Take the blessing of your mother and father

- Avoid meat and stick to a vegetarian meal

- Never accept any gift for free of cost, except for parents

- Donate dark red colored clothes

- Avoid eating salt on Sunday

- Wear Ruby

The Moon: Weak Moon in a chart indicates; mental illness, quickly bored and always looking for new excitement, pessimistic thoughts, always finding fault and making a complaint, bad relation with mother, always suspect the activities of spouse or lover, and frequent quarrel with them on any trivial matter, lack of control on mind, being easily attracted to useless items while shopping and making unnecessary purchases, lack of adjustment on new places, easily catch cough and cold, not able to keep any secret in mind and feel an urge to say anyone's matter to others.

Remedies for the Moon:

- Always respect your mother and never argue with her

- Turn off the television, computer, mobile, etc. at least one hour before going to sleep

- Meditate for a few minutes every morning

- Stop water leakage immediately from your house

- Stop passing one person's information to other

- Never discuss confidential things with anyone

- Feed Birds

- Wear Pearl

Mars: If Mars is weak; frequent cuts and minor wounds are possible, the problem of blood pressure, energy level low in the body, and always feel sleepy, a person easily gets angry and suffers from frequent headaches, ready to quarrel and always seek revenge, the problem of anemia and reproductive organs, females have a problem of abortions, problem-related with land, suffer minor or major accidents while traveling, dispute with siblings, face issues with police and frequent visit of the police station, hide here and there in fear of being caught.

Remedies for Mars:

- Chant Hanuman Chalisa daily

- Recite the Gayatri mantra daily

- Do not quarrel with anyone and do not fight on the streets

- Do not quarrel with siblings and always please them with gifts

- Maintain good relations with your family members and avoid leaving in nuclear families

- Donate blood occasionally

- Stop eating non-veg foods

- Wear Red Coral

Mercury: Weak mercury indicates; problems in communication, lack of analytical mind, wrong business decisions, low memory and the problem of forgetfulness, weak nervous system, skin-related problems, adolescence-onset sex problems and sex deviance, reduction of sexual strength, lack of focus on study, trying shortcuts in the examination, the problem of jealously with their friends, etc.

Remedies for Mercury:

- Quit alcohol

- Eat green vegetables

- Stop watching worthless movies and TV serials

- Don't argue with your friends and praise them for their success

- Wake up early

- Wear Emerald

Jupiter: Weak Jupiter indicates; excess fat in the body, lever-related problems, no interest in reading books, problem in education, no interest in religious activities, the problem with teachers, loss of gold, wrong charges of theft, diabetes, childless couple, etc.

Remedies for Jupiter:

- Read Vishnu Sahasranama Sthotram

- Eat turmeric

- Wear gold

- Spread knowledge and help students

- Read good books

- Take blessings for Guru and always respect

- Wear Yellow Sapphire or Pukhraj

Venus: Weak Venus indicates; beauty-related problems, unusual attraction toward the opposite sex, no support from females, quarrels with females, worthlessly buying fancy items and no control on expenditure, problem-related with reproductive organs, problem in the kidney, interest in pornography, always demanding attention, etc.

Remedies for Venus:

- Worship Lord Durga

- Always wear neat and clean cloths

- Never accept free gifts

- Eat cow ghee

- Do not eat foods with preservatives and chemicals

- Respect mother

- Do not argue with females and help her

- Wear Diamond

Saturn: Weak Saturn indicates; problems with labour, pessimistic thoughts, lack of vigor, always looking at the dark side, frequent change of servants and subordinates, unfaithful friends, servants or employees, always delay in work and never completing work on time, like to eat cold and stale foods, chronic diseases, etc.

Remedies for Saturn:

- Chant Shani Chalisa

- Always clean your body

- Always clean nearby surroundings where you live

- Always maintain balance in every situation and avoid overindulgence in any matter of life

- Avoid indulging in any type of court matter

- Donate footwear

- Wear Blue Sapphire

Rahu: Weak Rahu indicates; One is always afraid of snakes and always looks down to see if there is any snake, fingernails become weak and turn black, indulges in worthless quarrels often, no peace of his mind, and tendency to steal items, etc.

Remedies for Rahu:

- Chant Hanuman Chalisa

- Worship Lord Durga

- Never cheat any person

- Wear Hessonite or Gomeda stone

Ketu: Weak Ketu indicates; disbelief in religion, always trying to hide the face, diseases by bacteria, headless state of mind, lack of direction, unable to detect diseases easily, untruthful religious leader, etc.

Remedies for Ketu:

- Worship Lord Ganesha

- Do spiritual activities

- Donate blanket

- Feed street dogs and never beat them

- Wear Cat's Eye stone

Chapter 14

The Journey of Life: From Sun to Saturn

Human life is a journey that everyone undertakes after taking birth on this planet earth. The planets in our planetary system follow a sequence, some are small, some are large, they have different sizes and speeds, and they move around the Sun. There is an important meaning behind this planetary system and it is associated with human life. The Sun represents the soul, Saturn represents death and the journey from the Sun to Saturn is undertaken by each individual.

14.1 The Phase of Mercury

The first planet Mercury is very small in size and a very fast-moving planet. This represents the age of our childhood. Children are very active and nimble. They keep moving here and there and it is difficult for them to sit in one place for a longer time. They easily mingle with other children and easily laugh without any reason. Their small body, playfulness, and agility represent the Mercurian phase. The phase of Mercury lasts up to the age of 14 years.

14.2 The Phase of Venus

The next planet is Venus which is bigger in size than Mercury and a little smaller than Earth. Now the Mercurian phase has crossed and the children have grown up. They start to take interest in other-worldly affairs. The charm of Venus starts coming at this stage and they feel attraction toward the opposite sex. They want to enjoy life and takes interest in Venusian pursuits. They look for their partner, get married, and want to live life to the fullest. The phase of Venus lasts up to the age of 28 years.

14.3 The Phase of Mars

Now the journey moves towards Mars. Now the person becomes a mature person full of Martian energy. A person requires energy to run behind the desires and the planet of energy forces us to run and overcome obstacles. In this stage, the person shows determination, courage, and enthusiasm, and is not afraid of any kind of impediments. The energy level is high at this stage and people run here and there to fulfill their desires. The energy of Mars can be easily influenced by two planets - the first is Jupiter and the second is the shadow planet Rahu.

If it is influenced by Jupiter then the person gets the proper direction to utilize the energy. When energy gets direction, it gives fruitful results. If it is affected by Rahu then the person uses mischievous and criminal activities to fulfill his desires. The phase of Mars lasts up to the age of 42 years.

14.4 The Phase of Jupiter

Now the journey enters the Jupiter phase. In this state, the influence of the largest planet of the solar system starts coming and the person's body gradually becomes heavy. Many of them take interest in religious activities. Many people are skeptics and atheists when life passes through the phase of Mars. They do not believe in religion at all and do not want to do any kind of spiritual activities.

The tamasic planet Mars represents the person who moves only to fulfill his materialistic desire. But when the Jupiter phase starts many skeptics and atheist change their faith and start taking interest in religious activities. Many of them start doing charity, they start taking interest in books and other scriptures. The phase of Jupiter lasts up to the age of 56 years.

14.5 The Phase of Saturn

With the passage of time, the journey that started from the Sun reaches Saturn. The tendency of these two planets is completely opposite. Sun is hot and Saturn is cold, Sun represents life and

Saturn represents death. One who has taken birth will die one day. In Hindu mythology, Saturn is the son of the Sun, representing death comes from life. The phase of Saturn starts after the age of 56 years and lasts till the death of the person.

On the very first day of the person's birth, his journey towards Saturn starts. The journey from the Sun to Saturn – life to death every person is doing. When a child takes birth, everyone feels rejoice and movement starts, a new journey begins, but when a person dies his body becomes cold and still in one place. In India, when a person dies, people keep his body on top of large pieces of ice for some time. The journey from the Sun to Saturn has been completed.

But this is not the end, in Hindu culture, we burn the body, the cold has turned hot again.... and the journey continues.

Bibliography

Brihat Parashara Hora Sastra by Maharshi Parasara

Uttara Kalamrita by Kalidas

Bhrigu Sanhita, Translation by Bhagwandas Mittal, Rupesh Thahur Prasad Prakashan, Varanasi, India

Mansagari, Translation by Shree Sitaram Jha, Shree Thakur Prasad Pustak Bhandar, Varanasi, India

Brihat Jatak, Translation by Prof. P.S. Sastri, Rajan Publications, New Delhi

Jatak Parijat, Translation by V. Subramanya Sastri, Rajan Publications, New Delhi

Bhavartha Ratnakar, Translation by B.V. Raman, UBS Publishers, New Delhi,

Studies in Jaimini Astrology, Translation by B.V. Raman, MLBD, Delhi

Three Hundred Important Combination by B.V. Raman, MLBD, Delhi

ABC of Indian Astrology, Prof. (Dr.) Nimai Banerjee, Published by Mrs. Kanti Banerjee, Cuttak

Yogas in Astrology, Dr. K.S. Charak UMA Publications, Delhi

Astrology for 21st Century, Prash Trivedi, Alpha Publication, Delhi

Fundamental Principals of Astrology, by Prof. K.S. Krishnamurti

Fundamentals of Vedic Astrology by Bepin Behari

Myths and Symbols of Vedic Astrology by Bepin Behari

Gochar Phaladeepika by Dr. U.S Pulippani

Hindu Science of the Future by Harihar Majumder

Scientific Hindu Astrology Vol 1 &2 by P.S. Sastri

Solar system exploration<https://solarsystem.nasa.gov/planets/mars/in-depth/> Accessed on 6th Feb 2022

Welcome to starchild<https://starchild.gsfc.nasa.gov/docs/StarChild/StarChild.html> Accessed on 16th Feb 2022

COSMOS - The SAO Encyclopedia of Astronomy<https://astronomy.swin.edu.au/cosmos/> Accessed on 16th Feb 2022

Swami Vivekananda Quotes<https://quotefancy.com/> Accessed on 17th Feb 2022

Zodiac <https://www.britannica.com/topic/zodiac> Accessed on 10th Feb 2022

Obliquity<https://earthobservatory.nasa.gov/> - Accessed on 10th Feb 2022

How the Ecliptic and the Zodiac Workhttps://www.space.com/5417-ecliptic-zodiac-work.html > Accessed on 9th Feb 2022

About The Author

Ajay Srivastava is the founder of lotuswisdom.in and holds 'Bachelor of Science' from Deen Dayal Upadhyay Gorakhpur University, Gorakhpur (UP) and 'Masters Programme in International Business' from PSG Institute of Management, Coimbatore (Tamil Nadu).

He has over two decades of experience in the capital market as a Lead Analyst, Investment Banker, Consultant, and Advisor in identifying investment opportunities and formulating strategies. In his career, he has written various research notes and has done in-depth research from a commercial and financing point of view in multiple deals. With diverse industry experience and wide understanding, he started imparting his knowledge in the industry since 2013.

He has deep knowledge of graphology and very much interested in analyzing a person by handwriting and has analyzed the handwriting of hundreds of persons in his life.

He is very much passionate to learn about astrology and palmistry in deep and has completed 'JyotirVid' and 'JyotirVisharad' in Astrology from Bharatiya Vidya Bhavan, Mumbai. His various research articles have been published in the renowned Indian magazines "The Astrological eMagazine" and "Planets & Forecast".

Email ID: ajay.vastav@gmail.com

Web Site: http://www.lotuswisdom.in/

Blog: https://lotuswisdomonline.blogspot.com/

Books Written by the Author

1. Psychology and Investment

2. Vedic Astrology: The Light of Wisdom

3. Midlife Crisis: An Astrological Appraoch

4. Jupiter: The Planet of Fortune

5. The Joy of Creation and Success

6. The Light of Nakshatras

7. Sun: The Supreme Creator

8. Astrology & Predictions

9. Animal Symbols of Nakshatras

10. Astrology & Profession

11. Rahu & Ketu: The Invisible & Mysterious Planets

12. Planets & Human Life

Astrology Courses

1. Vedic Astrology for Beginners {Level – 1 (Basics)}

Module – 1: Basics of Astrology

Introduction; The Zodiac; Elements

Module – 2: Signs

Meaning of the Signs, Elements of the Signs, Qualities of the Signs, Odd and Even Signs, Sheershodaya & Prishtodaya Signs, Direction, Colors, Caste, Fruitful and Barren Signs, Masculine & Feminine Signs, Places, Other Major Qualities

Module – 3: Houses

Meaning of the 12 Houses, Types and Classifications of Houses

Module – 4: Planets

Planets and their Characteristics, Planetary Relationship, Exaltation, Debilitation & Mooltrikona, Natural Karakas, Karakas in Jaimini Astrology

Module – 5: Planets in Groups

Natural Benefic and Malefic Planets, Gender; Color; Caste; Guna and Places; Planet and Tastes; Nature of Planet; Elements; Metals; Age; Cloth and Height; Vegetable and Fruits; Physical Constituents and Tendency; Maturity Age of Planets; Planetary Aspects; Seasons

Module – 6: Planetary Strengths and Weaknesses

Strength of Planets based on its degrees, Direction; Direction Strength; Maran Karaka Sthana; Yog Karaka; Vargottam Planet; Shadabala

Module – 7: Retrograde and Combust Planet, Gandanta

2. <u>Vedic Astrology for Beginners {Level – 2 (Advanced)}</u>

Module 1: Vimshottari Dasha System

Nakshatra and Planetary Lordship, Change of Dasa and Results

Module 2: Basics of Nakshatra

Deity, Animal Symbol, Caste, Activity, Gana, Guna, Gender

Module 3: Important Yogas

Know the 30 most important astrological combinations

Module 4: Ashtakvarga

Interpretation of Ashtakvarga Table

Module 5: Transit of Planets and their impact

Understand the effect of transit of Jupiter, Saturn, Rahu–Ketu

Module 6: Planets and Profession

Identify the influence of the planet and the direction of profession

Module 7: Weak Planets and Remedies

Identify the signal of weak planets and useful remedies

Module 8: Key Steps to Chart Interpretation

Course Offerings:

   · 30 hours of live sessions (Level 1 & Level 2)

   · Learn various astrological concepts with practical examples

   · Mode - Online Classes

   · Recordings available

3. <u>Nakshatra Course</u>

Knowledge of Nakshatra is very important in astrology, without it one cannot understand how energy works and what will be the result of the transit of planets. Do not limit yourself to the movement of planets, explore the world of Nakshatra and understand the hidden secrets.

What You'll Learn

• How the knowledge of Nakshatra helps to understand the characteristics and negative traits of the person

• Effect of transit of planets and time of activation

• Meaning of each symbol and its influence

• Influence of the associated animal on the personality of the person

• When to start a new venture and when not to go ahead

• Related Profession

• Understand each concept with logic

Course Offerings:

• 60 hours of live sessions

• Learn various astrological concepts with practical examples

• Mode - Online Classes, Recordings available

• Medium - English

Contact Us:

Mobile No.: +91 9867837184

Email ID: ajay.vastav@gmail.com

Blog: https://lotuswisdomonline.blogspot.com/

<h1 style="text-align:center">4. <u>A Course on Animal Symbols of Nakshatras</u></h1>

In the ancient scriptures, a total of 14 animals are related to the 27 nakshatras, and the behavior of every person is limited to these 14 animals. To understand the various merits and demerits of a person, it is necessary to understand the different characteristics of these animals.

How to Utilize Such Knowledge

• You will be surprised to know that these animals decide whom we form a relationship in our life.

• These animals determine our relationships with our friends, our spouse, our partners, our juniors and superiors.

• This knowledge helps to channelize your energy in pursuit of higher goals in life.

• The human mind is a very complex creation and it is difficult to say why a person behaves in a certain way and why his behavior changes. Knowledge of animal traits can provide proper guidance in this regard.

Course Offerings:

· 30 hours of live sessions

· Learn various astrological concepts with practical examples

· Mode – Online Classes

· Recordings available

Sun:
The
Supreme
Creator
A Research Work on
Astrological Aspects of the Sun
Ajay Srivastava

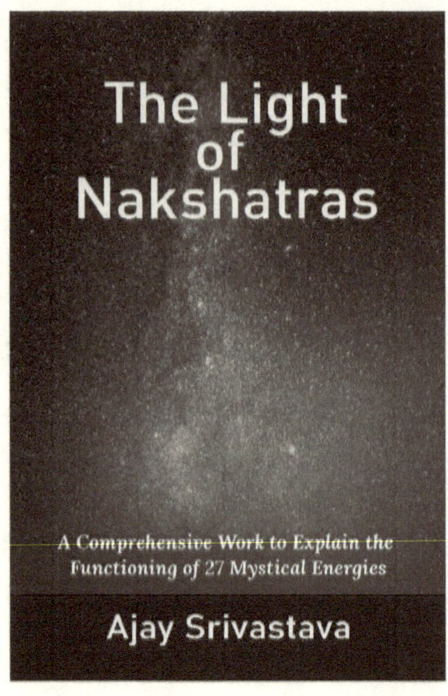

The Light
of
Nakshatras
A Comprehensive Work to Explain the
Functioning of 27 Mystical Energies
Ajay Srivastava

Jupiter:
The
Planet of
Fortune
Ajay Srivastava

Vedic Astrology
The Light of Wisdom
Astrology for Beginners,
Learn the Language of Stars
Ajay Srivastava

PSYCHOLOGY
AND
INVESTMENT
The Art of Investing in Stocks with an
Explanation of Human Psychology
AJAY SRIVASTAVA

The Joy
of
Creation and Success
Ajay Srivastava

Midlife
Crisis: An
Astrological
Approach
Understand The Timing Of Crisis,
Learn How To Turn A Crisis Into An Opportunity
Ajay Srivastava

Astrology
&
Predictions
Ajay Srivastava

Animal Symbols
of
Nakshatras
Ajay Srivastava

Astrology
&
Profession
Astrological Principles Behind Career
Selection, Downfall and Resurrection
Ajay Srivastava

Rahu & Ketu
The Invisible and Mysterious Planets
An Extensive Research Work to Demystify
the Mystery of Lunar Nodes
Ajay Srivastava

Planets
&
Human Life
Ajay Srivastava

Notes

<u>Notes</u>

www.ingramcontent.com/pod-product-compliance
Lightning Source LLC
Chambersburg PA
CBHW021155160726
47994CB00001B/227

9789356559882